With Trotsky in Exile

With Trotsky

FROM PRINKIPO

Jean van Heijenoort

HARVARD UNIVERSITY PRESS

Cambridge, Massachusetts, and London, England · 1978

in Exile

TO COYOACÁN

Library of Congress Cataloging in Publication Data

Van Heijenoort, Jean, 1912-
    With Trotsky in exile.

    Includes index.
    1. Trotskiĭ, Lev, 1879-1940.   2. Revolutionists—
Russia—Biography.   3. Statesmen—Russia—Biography.
4. Van Heijenoort, Jean 1912-   5. Secretaries—
Biography.   I. Title.
DK254.T6V36   947.084'092'4 [B]   78-935
ISBN 0-674-80255-1

FOREWORD

I lived for seven years with Leon Trotsky, from October 1932 to November 1939, with only a few interruptions. Having been a member of his political organization, I became his secretary, translator, and bodyguard. This little book is not a political history of that period. Nor is it a full-length portrait of the man. Rather, it is a book of recollections, which attempts to recreate the atmosphere in which Trotsky lived and worked during his years of exile.

I have tried not to rehearse what is already known, making an exception only when necessary in order to explain the narrative. I therefore ask of readers a certain knowledge of the events of those years. And I ask them to keep a sense of proportion, for the narrative often includes minor details known only to me which I do not want to be lost, but which should not be allowed to obscure the larger context. Knowing the past as I do, as well as the archives, it is my hope that these bits of information may some day allow a scholar to uncover a fact or identify a document.

What has been written on Leon Trotsky since his death, even by persons of good will, contains a fair amount of material error. In the Appendix I have tried to correct some of these errors. But often the text itself is written as a corrective to published items that I consider erroneous. I have dwelt most on the least-known episodes or on incidents that have been seriously distorted, trying in those cases to give all the details I can remember. The errors that have become so frequent are often nothing but careless, sometimes silly, mistakes. In other cases the Stalinist calumnies against Trotsky, which were both plentiful and persistent, have left their traces. But Trotsky as a personage also seems destined to give rise to mythogenic activities. Against all of these circumstances I thought it best to react by making my narrative as precise and concrete as possible.

I know the pitfalls of memory only too well and do not imagine that there are no mistakes in my narrative. But I kept some notes during my time with Trotsky, and later had at my disposal the archives, which I myself put in order. I have checked and rechecked many things. I did not think it advisable to combine these recollections with a critical examination of the personality of Leon Trotsky, of his ideas or his character. That would be another task.

The archives contain, for the period 1929 to 1940 alone, some twenty-two thousand documents, and other documents will surely turn up. Among the documents, there are some four thousand letters written by Trotsky, who was a great correspondent in quantity as well as style. All these remain to be exploited.

Until today, the writings of Trotsky have, almost without exception, been the subject of either complete anathematization or devout veneration. What these texts need is critical study—study of the ideas and their connections, of the arguments used, of the tacit assumptions, of the perspectives and their changes. They also require literary criticism, with an eye to style and metaphor, which could lead to insights into the personality of the author. These too are jobs that remain to be done.

Too often in the past I have described some episode from my life with Trotsky, only to find my interlocutor drawing conclusions quite different from those I intended. The power of words has its limits. I have tried to pick mine here with care, but I have no illusions. There will undoubtedly be misunderstandings, for a lived experience cannot be passed on like an object. Its communication is a reconstruction for the writer and sometimes a different one for the reader. Because I wrote the original text in French, my native language, and subsequently translated it into English, I beg the reader's further indulgence on that score.

This being said, here is my story.

CONTENTS

ILLUSTRATIONS

With Trotsky in Exile

1. PRINKIPO

I arrived in Prinkipo, Turkey, on October 20, 1932. I was twenty years old, having just ended nine years of confinement in French schools, and I was in total revolt against society.

Since the age of fifteen I had considered myself a communist, first with a Rousseauist and utopian tinge, then, in the midst of the great depression and its consequences, with a more directly political and activist attitude. As of the spring of 1932 I was considered a member of the Ligue communiste, the French Trotskyite group. At that time there were no membership cards. We were so few; hardly twenty or so were really active. But I took part in the activities of the group, which consisted mostly in carrying on discussions and in selling *La Vérité,* the weekly published by the group, at subway stations in the evening when the workers were coming home from work, or in the streets of working-class districts on Sunday morning. At night we would put up posters, and often ended up at a police station, since we had no money to put the required stamps on the posters. I was the first member of the Ligue who had not passed through the Communist party or the Young Communist League; all those whom I met there had been expelled from an official Communist organization.

The Ligue had been created in 1930 and had had a turbulent life. In 1932 its leadership was in the hands of two groups, Raymond Molinier and Pierre Frank on one side, Pierre Naville and Gérard Rosenthal on the other. The first group, endorsed by Trotsky, had the upper hand. The differences in temper and disposition between Molinier and Naville were a constant source of conflict. In 1930 there had been a flare-up that threatened the very existence of the new organization; peace had been imposed by Trotsky. When I joined the Ligue, there were no substantial political differences between the two camps, and the inner life of the organization was relatively quiet. But the antagonism between Molinier and Naville was to dominate the life of the Ligue during the years to come.

The French Trotskyite group was part of the international Trotskyite movement. Since 1923, Trotsky had criticized the leadership of the Communist International for what he considered deviations from the revolutionary path. But even after he was expelled from Russia by Stalin in 1929, his goal was to put the Communist International back on the revolutionary track, not to create a rival organization. Though formally expelled from the ranks of the official organization, the Trotskyites considered themselves as forming an opposition, called the Left Opposition, which for the time was outside but would some day find its place again within the ranks of the Communist International. "Our ideas will become your ideas and will express themselves in the program of the Communist International," Trotsky had once written.

In mid-1932, the main bone of contention between the Trotskyites and the Stalinists was the situation in Germany. Hitler was on the rise, and the two large working-class parties, the Social Democratic and the Communist, with their millions of votes remained divided and inert. The German Communist party, on Stalin's orders, was refusing common action with the Socialists, holding them no better than the Nazis. At the beginning of 1932, Stalin had made the profound discovery that Nazism and Social Democracy were "twins." The German Communist party's activity rested on the theory that the Socialists were actually "Social Fascists." An official Communist publication declared in July 1931: "All the forces of the [German Communist] party must be thrown into the struggle against the Social Democrats." The danger that Hitler represented was minimized, and several times the leadership of the German Communist party actually announced that the Nazi movement was on the verge of disintegration. Trotsky sounded the alarm. He denounced the senseless policy of the German Communist party in a stream of articles and pamphlets, full of wit and verve. From today's perspective, these writings shine out as the most brilliant of all he produced during his exile.

In July 1932 the situation in Germany suddenly grew worse, with a further shift to the right. In an attempt to justify the unjustifiable policy of the German Communist party and the Communist International, the French Communist party called a mass meeting, to be held on July 27 at

Bullier in Paris. Bullier was a large and popular dance-hall at the end of the Boulevard Saint-Michel, which could hold several thousand persons and was used from time to time for political meetings. The Ligue decided to be heard, to explain once more that the Socialist and Communist organizations should form a united front against Hitler. The hall was packed. Perhaps twenty of us stood in the midst of the crowd. After one or two speeches by official speakers of the Communist party, who repeated that the main enemy in Germany was the Social Democratic party, we opened fire. Raymond Molinier shouted, "We demand the floor for a five-minute declaration!" He added a few words about the seriousness of the situation in Germany and the necessity of a united front against Hitler, but he did not get far. At a sign from Pierre Sémard, a leader of the French Communist party who had made a specialty of persecuting the Trotskyites, the attendants, who had already taken positions around us, closed in, grabbed some chairs, and started to club us. I was one of the more seriously injured; my friends dragged me out with a bloody head.

In June Molinier had asked me if I was willing to go to the island of Prinkipo, to be Trotsky's secretary. Somebody was needed, and one of the reasons for Molinier's choice was no doubt the fact that I could read Russian, which I had taught myself. My departure was postponed several times. Finally on October 13, 1932, I left Marseilles aboard the *Lamartine,* and after stops in Naples and Piraeus I landed at Istanbul on the morning of October 20. Later I learned that Pierre Frank, who was then in Prinkipo, had come to fetch me, but in my hurry I went down the plank so fast that he missed me. Without leaving the pier, I immediately took the small paddle boat for Prinkipo, where I landed at the end of the morning, suitcase in hand. When I arrived at the gate of the house, I gave a note to the Turkish policeman stationed there. Jan Frankel came to greet me. I was chatting with him in the entrance hall when Trotsky came down from his study, wearing a suit of white linen. Turning to Jan, he said, "He looks like Otto." That was Otto Schüssler, who was then living in the house; he was blond, like me, but there the likeness ended, for we were quite different in height and features.

Trotsky was now fifty-two. His appearance, well known to me from his pictures, was striking. Upon first meeting him in 1929, Jeanne Martin, who was married to Raymond Molinier, had told Trotsky, "You look like

Trotsky and Natalia Ivanovna Sedova
at the time of their arrival in Turkey, 1929.

your pictures," to which he replied, "That's embarrassing; it is as if one were a piece of furniture." Yet Trotsky was far from being a piece of furniture. The liveliness of his gestures and the vivaciousness of his speech drew immediate attention. What struck one first was his forehead, lofty and straight even though not yet heightened by baldness. After that his eyes, blue and deep, with a gaze both powerful and sure of that power. (During his later stay in France, Trotsky at times had to travel incognito in order to simplify the problem of guarding him. He shaved off his goatee and brushed his hair to one side, dividing it by a part; but when it came to his leaving the house and mingling with the public, I always worried: "No, it's really impossible. The first passerby will recognize him. He can't change that gaze of his.") Then when Trotsky began to talk, what attracted attention was his mouth. Whether he spoke in Russian or a foreign language, his lips shaped the words clearly and distinctly. He was irritated at others' confused and hasty speech and forced himself to enunciate with precision. Only when he was addressing Natalia in Russian did his enunciation on occasion become more hurried and less articulate, sometimes dropping to a whisper. When in conversation with visitors in his study, his hands, at first resting on the edge of the work table, would soon begin to move with wide, firm gestures, as though aiding his lips in molding the expression of his thought. The set of his head with its halo of hair and indeed the whole carriage of his body were proud and stately. He had an above-medium build, with a powerful chest and a broad, stalwart back, but his musculature was slight and his legs, by comparison with his chest, appeared slender. One day later in Mexico in a playful moment, he measured himself against me. He was exactly one centimeter shorter than I, and thus between five feet ten and five feet eleven.

In the fall of 1920 a British sculptress, Clare Sheridan, a cousin of Winston Churchill, had gone to Moscow to do heads of various Bolshevik leaders. She later remarked in her memoirs that Trotsky "pointed out to me how unsymmetrical his face is. He opened his mouth and snapped his teeth to show me that his underjaw is crooked." Yet these defects were not apparent. Sheridan added that his "nose is also crooked and looks as though it has been broken." When she asked him to take off his pince-nez, because it hampered her, he "hated doing this, he says he feels 'désarmé' and absolutely lost without them. It seemed akin to physical pain, taking them off—they have become part of him and the loss of them completely changes his individuality. It is a pity, as they rather spoil an otherwise classical head." During all the years I was to be with Trotsky, I would see him without his glasses only two or three times at most, for he hardly ever took them off in the presence of persons other than Natalia. Without the glasses, which were quite strong, his eyes seemed smaller and more closely set.

When I first met Trotsky in Prinkipo, he showed no outward sign of the series of ordeals that had brought him to this point. The journey had begun in 1923, when he first began to struggle against Stalin inside the Russian Communist party. Four years later he was expelled from the party and stripped of all official functions. At the beginning of 1928 Stalin deported him to Alma Ata, the main city of Kazakhstan, in eastern Soviet Central Asia, some two thousand miles from Moscow. Trotsky was accompanied by his second wife, Natalia, and their elder son, Liova, who was then twenty-two. Their younger son, Sergei, an engineer who was not involved in politics, remained in western Russia, where he continued to lead his own life. Although closely watched in Alma Ata by the G.P.U. (the Soviet secret service), Trotsky still had a certain freedom. He received mail and went hunting. Trotsky once told me, however, that while in Alma Ata, Liova and he had studied maps showing the route to the Chinese border, about one hundred and sixty miles away, for a possible escape in that direction.

By the end of 1928 Stalin had come to the conclusion that Trotsky could no longer stay in Alma Ata. To kill Trotsky at that time would have aroused opposition on the part of some members of the Politburo and could have enraged a young Trotskyite to the point of making an attempt on Stalin's life. To exile him seemed to be the way out. Yet for a long time Stalin hesitated. The train that was carrying Trotsky, Natalia, and Liova from Alma Ata back to western Russia stood for twelve days and nights on a side track, waiting for orders. Stalin finally made up his mind, and Trotsky was taken to Istanbul. Stalin had probably speculated that, once abroad, Trotsky would remain isolated, with no friends and no money, and could be discredited in the eyes of the Russian people if he published articles in the foreign newspapers.

Trotsky arrived in Istanbul from Odessa on February 12, 1929, with Natalia and Liova. They first lived in the Soviet consulate, where they found themselves in an ambiguous situation, at once guests and prisoners; the arrangement lasted only about three weeks. On March 5 they left the consulate and stayed a few days in the Tokatliyan Hotel on the main street of Pera. On March 6 Trotsky sent a cable to Maurice Paz, a lawyer, in Paris: FREE STAYING HOTEL SEEKING LODGINGS GREETINGS LEON. The opening word betrays Trotsky's feelings while in the Soviet consulate. The new émigrés then moved into a furnished apartment, found by Liova, in the section called Bomonti of the Shishli suburb of Istanbul, at number 29 Izzet Pasha Street. At the end of April they settled down on the island of Prinkipo in the villa Izzet Pasha (the fact that the street and the villa have the same name has misled some narrators). That villa was on the northern coast of the island, like the later house where I lived, but nearer the landing wharf. When the Izzet Pasha villa was damaged by fire on March 1, 1931, Trotsky moved for about four weeks to Prinkipo's small hotel, the Savoy. At the end of March he left Prinkipo and moved to Moda on the Asian coast, a suburb of the small town of Kadiköy. He lived at number

22 Shifa Street. Finally in January 1932 he went back to Prinkipo, to settle in the villa in which he was living when I joined him in October.

When I arrived, I found Jan Frankel from Prague, Pierre Frank from Paris, and Otto Schüssler from Leipzig also living in the house. A Russian typist, Maria Ilinishna Pevsner, who had an apartment in Istanbul, would come in the morning and leave at the end of the afternoon; when the sea was bad, she spent the night at the Savoy Hotel. Frankel, who had been in Prinkipo since April 15, 1930, had become the main secretary after Liova's departure on February 18, 1931, for Berlin to resume his studies in engineering and to take part in revolutionary politics. Schüssler, who had arrived in May 1932, was a member of the leadership of the German Trotskyite group, and Frank, who had arrived on July 15, 1932, was one of the leaders of the French Trotskyite group. Although both had come to Prinkipo not as secretaries but as visitors, their visits had been extended because there was so much work to be done. In practice, the differences between workers and guests were not pronounced. As for me, after a training period I was to take Frankel's place. The only other resident was Trotsky's grandson Vsievolod, or Sieva for short, who had been born in 1926. He and his mother Zinaida, or Zina for short, Trotsky's elder daughter by his first wife, had left Russia at the end of 1930 and arrived in Prinkipo to live on January 8, 1931. On October 22, 1931, Zina had followed Liova to Berlin in order to obtain medical treatment, leaving Sieva with Trotsky and Natalia in Turkey.

Prinkipo is the largest island in a small archipelago in the Sea of Marmara. This archipelago includes four main islands, which are inhabited, and five smaller ones, which are not. Of the inhabited islands, Prinkipo is the farthest from Istanbul. The distance is about twenty miles, and at that time the paddle boats that went from the Pera Bridge to the wharf in Prinkipo took about an hour and a half, including stops at the other islands, to complete the trip.

The island of Prinkipo is about eight miles in circumference. A large part of it was not then inhabited. The population was concentrated on the northeast coast in a village, almost a small town, near the wharf. Villas were spread out along the northern coast of the island, becoming rarer and rarer in the west, and the southwestern part of the island was uninhabited. As one moved from the coast inland, the ground rose

*Otto Schüssler, Jean van Heijenoort, and Pierre Frank
in the garden of the house at Prinkipo, early 1933.*

steeply. The highest spot was some six hundred feet above sea level, and near it was a Greek orthodox monastery. The interior of the island was covered with pines, which filled the air with their fragrance. The soil was reddish. At various times of day the sea and the sky took on vivid, ever-changing colors. At dawn and sunset these colors were purple and mauve, rarely seen anywhere else in the world.

To the east of the island, a few miles away, is the coast of Asia; to the northwest, much farther away and hardly visible, is the coast of Europe. Halki, which within the archipelago is the nearest inhabited island to Prinkipo, lies to the northwest at a distance of about a mile. The Sea of Marmara, with its islands and the Asian coast, the vegetation of Prinkipo, and the sky — all these formed the most beautiful site in the world. I saw Prinkipo again in 1973. The island is much more built up. The Asian coast, where there was in 1932 only the village of Kartal, is now a suburb of Istanbul, covered with houses. The Sea of Marmara is polluted, and a cement factory sends a continuous wreath of smoke from the Asian mainland into the sky above Prinkipo.

In 1932 the population of Prinkipo was mainly Greek, although the administration and the police were in the hands of the Turks. All the islands in the archipelago have both a Greek and a Turkish name. In Turkish, Prinkipo is called Büyük Ada, or Great Island. Prinkipo, or the Princes' Island, is the place where the emperor of Byzantium would relegate princes who were out of favor, often after having them blinded.

The villa occupied by Trotsky was on the northern coast, a fifteen-minute walk from the wharf, where houses were less frequent. The house, built forty or fifty years before, was solidly made and had undoubtedly been the summer residence of an important personage in Istanbul. It stood in the middle of a rectangular garden, which it divided into two parts, one on the street side, the other by the sea. The garden was surrounded by stone walls, some seven feet high. The house was reached through a dead-end street, Hamladji Sokagi, which ran down to the sea. After entering through a small iron gate, one found, on the right, a cabin where a small garrison of four to six Turkish policemen was permanently stationed. On the left, a path led to the main entrance of the house. The garden, rather neglected, was full of shrubs and flowers, and during the afternoon lizards basked in the sun on the walls. One could go through the house and out on the side facing the

The house on Hamladji Street in Prinkipo,
where Trotsky lived from January 1932 to July 1933.

sea. There the garden went down rapidly to the shore, and the path zig-
zagged amidst rich Mediterranean vegetation. At the end of the garden
was a gate which opened onto the private wharf of the house, solidly
built of heavy stones.

The house had two main storeys. On the ground floor, after the entrance hall, was a large central room, with big windows and glazed doors
facing the sea, which was used as the dining room. Near the entrance on
the left was a room used as a guard room, then a room that, when I arrived, was used by Pierre Frank and Otto Schüssler. On the right was
the kitchen. On the second floor, a large central corridor ended with a
balcony looking out on the sea. Against the walls on each side of this
corridor were shelves filled with books and folders. To the left of the
corridor was the bathroom used by Trotsky and Natalia, then their bedroom. On the right was, first, a room that served as bedroom and study
for Jan Frankel and myself, then a small office, which we called the
chancellery, where Maria Ilinishna worked, and finally in the corner
Trotsky's study, large and well-lighted, with windows on two sides. On
the third floor was an attic, where files of newspapers and magazines
were kept, and a room where the cook slept. There was no telephone in
the house. In case of need, we used the one in the Savoy Hotel, ten minutes away. The whole house was sparsely furnished. We seemed to camp
rather than live there. The walls were whitewashed. But the house was
roomy, dry, and full of light.

As soon as I moved in, I was quickly integrated into the life of the
household. An important activity, to which I had immediately to adapt
myself, was fishing. At the wharf at the foot of the garden were two fishing boats, each about sixteen feet long. One had an outboard motor. A
Greek fisherman, Kharalambos, who was young, simple-hearted, and
pure, took care of the boats and the fishing gear. We would leave at half
past four in the morning, when it was still dark. With a quick stride,
Trotsky descended the path that led from the house to the wharf. Sometimes, though rarely, Natalia came on these early fishing expeditions.
One or two of the secretaries always came along, as well as a Turkish
policeman. At the wharf, Kharalambos had everything prepared, and
we left quickly. Soon the sky began to take on a mauve tinge. Once at
sea, we started fishing with lines or nets — an activity that was sometimes
exhausting — by means of various techniques, which Kharalambos su-

Trotsky, Natalia, and Kharalambos fishing;
in the background is the western end of Prinkipo.

pervised, according to the time of year and the kinds of fish. The Sea of
Marmara was then teeming with fish, and we brought back great quan-
tities. Above all, there were red mullets and some very large fish that we
called palamuts, a kind of bonito, which have the form and colors of
mackerel but are much bigger; but there were many other kinds as
well. At meals, though we usually ate fish, we hardly made a dent in
what we had caught. We gave what was left to the Prinkipo hospital.

Sometimes Kharalambos would set lobster traps at the end of the afternoon, and the next morning we would go out to lift them. One day
we came back with some thirty lobsters, which with great pride Trotsky
asked us to lay out on the floor of the dining room. Sometimes we also
set baited lines in the evening; but sharks would get at these lines during
the night, and when we pulled in a line, a seven-foot monster would appear, which we had to shoot.

Before my arrival a number of fishing incidents had taken place, which became part of what one might call the folklore of the household. One day Jeanne Martin, who periodically worked as a secretary in Prinkipo, accompanied Trotsky fishing. A net full of fish was pulled in, and the poor creatures lay dying in the bottom of the boat. Jeanne, who had naturalist tendencies, started to throw the fish back into the sea by the armful. Needless to say, Trotsky did not relish that kind of behavior. Another incident that entered the folklore involved a motor failure during a fishing expedition far away near Yalova, which made it necessary to pitch camp on the Asian coast and to sleep under the stars.

From time to time, fishing gave place to hunting. We would go by boat to hunt on the Asian coast, near Kartal. After pulling the boat onto the beach and leaving it there in the charge of Kharalambos, we would follow the dog across a wild and shrubby terrain, a kind of bush. The game consisted almost exclusively of quail; rarely did we see a rabbit. Trotsky shot fast and accurately. But it was obvious that this kind of hunting engrossed him much less than fishing. Game was not abundant. The expedition often turned into a mere walk. Trotsky would never stop asking questions about the work in the house ("Have you answered that letter?" and so on), which was not the case when fishing. He would also tell hunting stories. For example, to hunt a wolf in Siberia, a peasant runs very fast in a large semicircle while reeling off a ball of string that has been coated with tallow, which the wolf will not cross. Trotsky also told how Lenin, when hunting, would drag along Zinoviev, who hated that kind of activity and as soon as he could would hide in a haystack, from which Lenin had to pull him out by the boots. We also had a few picnics in the countryside on the Asian coast. From one of these I came back so sunburnt that Natalia had to take care of my burns with yogurt, in the Russian manner.

After our early-morning fishing or hunting, we would return to the house at eight to have a quick, simple breakfast of tea and goat cheese. Natalia prepared the tea and poured it for everybody. When the brew was too hot, Trotsky poured it, in the Russian manner, from his cup into the saucer and then drank it from the saucer. To me, freshly arrived from France, this custom at first seemed strange.

After breakfast, Maria Ilinishna would arrive, and Trotsky began to dictate in Russian. The chancellery, where Maria Ilinishna sat at her typewriter, had a door that led into Trotsky's study. He would walk back and forth from his study to the chancellery, dictating all the while, if not in full voice, at least in resonant tones. Often this lasted till lunchtime. If I was in my room, I could hear his well-articulated sentences, rhythmical and melodious. One could guess what the power of this voice had been when addressing a crowd, at a time when the art of oratory was not yet aided by electronic devices.

When composing letters in other languages, he dictated while seated at his desk. He could handle French quite well, his main difficulties being with the subjunctive and conjunctions. He could certainly speak the language with great naturalness. At times in French his voice took on a sharp tone that it did not seem to have in Russian, the French *u* becoming almost *ee* and the French mute *e* becoming *ay*. He also dictated in German, and as far as I can judge, his syntax was better in German than in French, and so was his pronunciation. While Swabeck and then Shachtman were staying in Prinkipo in 1933, Trotsky wrote letters in English with their help. Later on, he greatly improved his English, and in Mexico he learned enough Spanish to read the newspapers and hold conversations.

Trotsky's writings in exile fall into three categories: correspondence, articles or pamphlets, and books. This tripartite classification is not absolute. Sometimes a text begun as a letter would acquire a title and become an article, or a pamphlet such as *What Next?* would come to be regarded as a book. The bulk of Trotsky's writings nevertheless fit into these major divisions.

The correspondence owed its existence largely to the number of Trotskyite groups that were active in about thirty countries. Each of these groups was usually divided into two or three factions, which were carrying on a sharp ideological or organizational struggle. As soon as Trotsky considered himself sufficiently informed about a particular struggle, he would intervene directly. Such interventions accounted for an important part of his correspondence. In Prinkipo, he dictated to Pierre Frank or me in French and to Otto Schüssler or Jan Frankel in German, and for correspondents who could read Russian, he dictated to Maria Ilinishna Pevsner. Every second or third day he dictated a long letter in Russian for Liova, who was then in Berlin. The correspondence was classified in folders kept in the chancellery.

Trotsky in his study at the Izzet Pasha villa, early 1931.

The articles were written in reaction to current political events. Trotsky rarely had two articles in progress at the same time. An article might be a short note or could grow to the point of becoming a pamphlet or small book. All of Trotsky's articles, except for some short articles written later under difficult circumstances, were dictated in Russian. Many were published in the *Bulletin of the Opposition*. Translated, they were published in the Trotskyite press throughout the world. In order to earn money, from time to time he sent an article of a more general character to a "bourgeois" publication in Germany (before Hitler's rise to power) or in the United States.

Trotsky's major books were *My Life, History of the Russian Revolution, The Revolution Betrayed, Lenin,* and *Stalin.* Work on these projects stretched over several months, sometimes over several years, and was carried on simultaneously with his other writings.

Before my arrival in Prinkipo, the translation of works from Russian to French for publication had been done in France by various persons. Maurice Parijanine had translated *My Life,* but the embellishments with which he adorned his translation and the footnotes that he added to Trotsky's text had led to contentions. Matters were eventually somewhat straightened out, and in the spring of 1932 Raymond Molinier sent Parijanine to Prinkipo for three weeks. After Trotsky explained to Parijanine on this visit that he wanted the translations of his writings to be precise and straightforward, without additions, he entrusted him with the translation of the *History.* Parijanine even, I believe, did part of this translation in Turkey, under Trotsky's supervision, before going back to Paris. By the time of my arrival, the proofs of the second volume were being corrected, and Trotsky was still finding Parijanine's translation too verbose. One of my first tasks, therefore, with Pierre Frank, was to remove the flourishes that Parijanine had added to Trotsky's prose. I also started to translate articles written by Trotsky. At first, I would read him a translation in his study, while he followed the Russian text. After a few weeks, he gave up this practice.

The morning's work ended at one o'clock or a bit before, when we had lunch. This meal never lasted more than half an hour. Ordinarily we drank only water, but a bottle of Dardanelles wine appeared on the table on November 7, the anniversary of both the October insurrection and Trotsky's birth. Besides fish, we sometimes had meatballs or stuffed tomatoes or peppers, but almost never butcher's meat. Trotsky was not a big eater. Moreover, he did not seem to pay any attention to what he ate. During the seven years that I had meals with him three times a day, seated at his right, I never heard him make a remark about the food. Although he could discuss the differences between French and American apples, he was not expressing personal tastes but was rather making general observations. Trotsky also did not smoke and would not tolerate smoking in his presence.

In the isolation of Prinkipo, closeted with a group of persons that remained unchanged for months, Trotsky did not always feel obliged to have animated conversation during meals. I remember meals at which he was so preoccupied that he did not utter a word. Otherwise his talk generally revolved around our work. He would comment on a piece of information received in a letter or read in a newspaper. Or he would try out on us some political observations which a few days later we often found incorporated in an article. Sometimes he would evoke memories. These included memories of his youth, like the occasion when he had made himself ridiculous at his cousin's house in Odessa by putting mustard on chicken. Sometimes they were memories from the Kremlin, where he had an apartment close to Lenin's. The memories came from each period of his life except one, the civil war. I often heard him speak generally of the civil war. He would compare some episode of it to the American Civil War or, later, to the Mexican civil war. But these remarks were always political observations. I never heard him recall memories of a personal character connected with the civil war.

Trotsky's remarks about individuals were most often sarcastic. Comments on his enemies and adversaries were so as a matter of course, but his sarcasm, transformed into friendly jesting, was frequently directed at those close to him as well. For example, when Daladier was head of the French government, Trotsky would start off a remark to me, "Your Daladier." Needless to say, I had no responsibility for Daladier. To an American in the house, he would say, "Your Roosevelt." His conversation often had this biting edge. After visiting Trotsky in Mexico in 1938, André Breton spoke of his "teasing" tone. Trotsky enjoyed giving names to those around him. I did not like tea, and after a while I succeeded in having milk at breakfast. Then I became Molokan, the Milk Drinker, from the name of the members of a Russian sect who lived on milk. One day, after managing to start up the water pump, I was baptized the Technocrat; it was in the spring of 1933, at a time when Technocracy was a brand-new fad. During the negotiations with the French consul in Istanbul concerning a French visa, I became known as the Minister of Foreign Affairs. Much later in Mexico, when I had come to know Trotsky's habits well and could anticipate his wishes, I became Uzhe, Already, a nickname that, I was told, Lenin gave to Sverdlov.

After lunch, Trotsky retired, and no one was permitted to disturb him for any reason, even the arrival of a cable. It was then that he read nonpolitical writings, quite often a Russian or French novel. Thus he began to read the long series of volumes of *Men of Good Will*, by Jules Romains, whom he called "an incomparable artist." After reading, he took a nap for perhaps twenty minutes, and his rest was over by four o'clock. Life then resumed in the house.

Every afternoon we all took tea together in the dining room, where we had the same kind of conversation as during lunch. Dinner, at seven, was light and short. After dinner, Trotsky again worked in his study and then retired to the bedroom at nine or half past. Generally he was not sleeping well, and often he had to take sleeping pills. Natalia would tell us in the morning, "L.D. had to take Nembutal again last night." Frankel told me that in 1930, during the bitter factional fights in the French Trotskyite group, if a cable arrived late in the day with news of a new turn in the struggle, he would conspire with Natalia to keep the cable from Trotsky until the following morning, after he had enjoyed an undisturbed night.

While Trotsky slept, one or more of us stood guard through the night, as we did during the day. Our concern was for Trotsky's life, which had been in increasing jeopardy since his first opposition to Stalin in 1923. By 1932 it may already have been apparent to Stalin that he had made a mistake in letting Trotsky out of Russia. Trotsky had found new friends abroad, was publishing the *Bulletin of the Opposition* in Russian, and was pouring out books, pamphlets, and articles. With the passing years the possibility was growing that Stalin would "correct" his mistake by assassinating Trotsky. There was a possible danger for Trotsky from still another quarter. In those years Istanbul teemed with White Russians, who had fought in the civil war and were hostile to Trotsky. In fact, the two threats could easily combine: through the G.P.U., Stalin might employ a White Russian to make an attempt on Trotsky's life.

In 1932-33, therefore, security was a constant care. Guard duty took much of our time. We were always armed. At the time we usually carried German Parabellums; later in Mexico we had Colts. Trotsky himself had a strange small pistol — where it came from I do not know. Whenever he came to the ground floor of the house for a meal, we closed some of the windows and doors with iron shutters, and one of us kept watch in the garden around the house. During the night, one of us stayed on duty in the guardroom near the entrance and at certain times made the rounds, occasionally with one of the Turkish policemen. I never deluded myself about the efficacy of our guard. When a large state, with massive financial and technical means at its disposal, wants to eliminate a single man, devoid of resources and surrounded by only a few young friends, the contest is wholly one-sided. We were doing what we could, thinking that

*Jean van Heijenoort on the balcony
of the house in Prinkipo, spring 1933.*

we might at least prevent an attack by an unbalanced person. In fact, a G.P.U. agent, Blumkin, who had been a member of Trotsky's military secretariat during the civil war and had met Liova in 1929 in a street of Istanbul, made a secret visit to Trotsky and warned him that at least twenty trained men were necessary to guarantee his safety. We were hardly three or four, and barely trained. Yet the difficulties never lessened our zeal and devotion.

The guard was exhausting, and we tried several different systems. One of them involved our taking turns every four hours; according to another schedule, one person remained on duty for twenty-four hours at a stretch. Nothing was ever satisfactory, for we were too few. To be awakened at two in the morning in order to take a turn of duty is hard to endure when it goes on month after month. The lack of sleep is one of my memories of Prinkipo. In the daytime, if one of us stretched out on his bed to read or nap and Trotsky happened to enter the room, he never failed to exclaim, "Here is the Russian emigration!"

Every morning except Friday, which was then a holiday in Turkey, the mailman brought a large amount of mail. Letters, newspapers, books, packages of documents would come from all over the world. We opened all packages before giving them to Trotsky, but letters were not opened, for at that time the techniques of assassination, we thought, did not include the possibility of putting a deadly device in a small envelope. Every day there were letters from cranks; some quoted from the Bible, others sent recommendations to Trotsky for maintaining his health or saving his soul. And there were always the autograph collectors.

The mail also brought us newspapers from western Europe after a delay of two or three days. Trotsky regularly read *Le Temps* and *Die deutsche allgemeine Zeitung,* underlining passages with his blue and red pencils. Some articles were cut out and classified in folders for his future writing. Every morning we received the Turkish daily newspapers, whose titles, at least, we could decipher. Every afternoon one of us went to the wharf to buy the small afternoon newspapers in French and German that were published in Istanbul and gave us the dispatches from the international news services.

Our relations with the people of Prinkipo were minimal. There was a Greek cook, who slept in the house. A Greek cleaning woman would

come in the morning. At the time of Trotsky's first installation at Prinkipo in 1929, an attempt had been made, for reasons of security, to do
without outside help. But the plan soon had to be abandoned, because
we couldn't handle the work. Here is what Jeanne Martin wrote to me
on this point in a letter dated February 25, 1959: "When I arrived in the
villa, Raymond asked me if, in addition to a certain amount of secretarial work (reading and clipping foreign newspapers — I had chosen to
work on the English ones), I would also like to cook for everybody, with
Natalia's help. He explained to me that it was impossible, for reasons of
security, to engage any paid help, especially for cooking, as you would
understand. I accepted. My role was somewhat delicate, difficult, and
burdensome. For L.D. would demand that the clippings to be given to
him as quickly as possible (we went through all the newspapers, you remember, that came from Europe); on the other hand, I had to take
upon myself almost everything that had to do with buying food in the
market and preparing the meals, and because of the strict diet that was
medically imposed upon L.D., two different kinds of meals had to be
prepared; all that with the primitive facilities, and meals had to be
served at exactly the time fixed, since L.D.'s schedule was very strict, as
you know. One day I saw him go back up to his study and later refuse to
come down again because he had not found lunch ready at the pre-
scribed time. He would not wait to be called; he would come down and
it had to be ready. He did not say a word, for he never complained. But
Natalia and I were desperate." Clearly the system could not work, and
help had to be hired.

We had neither friends nor acquaintances in the Turkish world. Our
only relations in Istanbul were with the landlord, an Armenian to whom
we paid the rent every month, and a few shopkeepers from whom we
bought stationery and fishing gear. During my stay in Prinkipo, Trotsky
went once or twice to Istanbul to see a dentist. We then hired a motor
launch, which came to the wharf of the house and took us directly to
Istanbul.

Throughout Trotsky's stay in Turkey there were no difficulties with
the Turkish authorities. During the Turkish struggle for national inde-
pendence in 1920 Kemal Pasha had received arms from Soviet Russia,
which had been delivered through the agency of Trotsky as commissar
of war. Years later, a visitor reported Trotsky as having said in 1933:

"When Turkey was fighting Greece in the war I helped Kemal Pasha with the Red Army. Fellow soldiers don't forget such things. That was why Kemal Pasha didn't lock me up in spite of pressure from Stalin." The words may not be exactly Trotsky's, but he did in fact give military supplies. I also heard it said that in the early years of the Russian Revolution, Lenin and Trotsky had been made honorary members of the Turkish Parliament.

In September 1965 Gérard Rosenthal told me of an incident that had occurred at the beginning of 1930 during a visit of his to Trotsky in Prinkipo, where he stayed for about two months. One day Kemal Pasha came to visit an official, perhaps a minister, who had a villa in Prinkipo near the villa Izzet Pasha, where Trotsky was then living. Kemal Pasha sent an aide-de-camp to ask whether Trotsky would receive him. In order to dodge the meeting, Trotsky answered that he was not well. The probable reason is that Trotsky did not want to have any personal contact with Kemal Pasha, who was then persecuting the Turkish Communists. As far as I know, this was the only attempt at communication between high Turkish authorities and Trotsky.

When Trotsky wanted to leave Turkey in November 1932 to give a lecture in Copenhagen, the Turkish authorities gave Turkish passports for aliens to Trotsky and Natalia without any difficulty. Their Soviet passports had expired and could not be renewed, since Trotsky and his family had been deprived of their Soviet citizenship by a decree of February 20, 1932. Upon their return from Copenhagen, they were allowed to settle down again in Prinkipo without any problem, and the Turkish passports were used again when they left for France in July 1933. In fact, these passports, which had long since expired, were the only identification papers that Trotsky and Natalia later had to enter Norway and then Mexico. The Turkish authorities also granted visas without any difficulty whenever necessary to persons who wanted to visit Trotsky in Turkey or even to stay there for a time, like myself. It was enough to say that one was visiting Trotsky on matters related to publishing or translating.

In Prinkipo, aliens had to register with the local police. For persons living in Trotsky's house, this was always done quite simply. Omer Effendi, commander of the garrison of Turkish policemen at the gate of the house, spoke Russian as well as some French, which was probably the reason he had been chosen. He was a Caucasian, and one evening in a mood of confidence he hummed for me, low enough not to be heard by the other policemen, a song that began, "Ia ni Russki, ia ni Turtski, ia Kavkavski [I am not a Russian, I am not a Turk, I am a Caucasian]."

Thus our relations with the Turkish authorities were correct, though nothing more. We did not have close enough contact with high officials to settle small affairs, as would later be the case in Mexico. When Arne Swabeck, a leader of the American Trotskyite organization, arrived in Prinkipo in 1933, for example, he brought from Berlin a short-wave receiver, given to him for us by Liova. At the border the receiver was taken away from him by the customs officers. After spending two days at the Istanbul customs house in vain negotiations with the Turkish authorities, I finally had to leave with an empty suitcase.

With Trotsky's arrival in Turkey, a flow of visitors had begun to come from Western Europe. The first of these was the French lawyer Maurice Paz, who arrived on March 12 or 13, 1929, and stayed a few days. He was one of the leaders in Paris of an opposition group that was publishing the magazine *Contre le courant*. The political discussions between Trotsky and Paz quickly turned sour. Moreover, Paz could not forget that he was a lawyer. Apparently he even asked Trotsky for reimbursement for his travel expenses. Trotsky was looking for another kind of man. At one point Paz recommended a certain brand of ink which Trotsky, who was forever preoccupied with his pen and everything else involved with the act of writing, found acceptable and adopted. "It was the only good thing he ever did," Trotsky later said of Paz's recommendation.

At the end of March 1929, a young stranger arrived from Paris. On April 20 Trotsky wrote to Paz: "Personally, Raymond Molinier is one of the most obliging, practical, and energetic men that one can imagine. He has found a place for us to live, discussed the conditions with the landlady, and so on. He is quite ready to stay with us for a few months, with his wife." Molinier had indeed won Trotsky's esteem. A few months later Trotsky told a visitor, "Raymond Molinier is the prefiguration of the future communist revolutionary." Molinier went back to Paris in May, but his wife, Jeanne, whose maiden name was Martin des Pallières, stayed on for a while in Prinkipo.

Alfred and Marguerite Rosmer, old friends of the Trotskys, arrived shortly before mid-May, 1929. Rosmer had known Trotsky in Paris during World War I and had met him again in Russia during the early twenties. Marguerite stayed four weeks, Alfred till mid-July. During this period the Rosmers started to play the role of mediators between Trotsky and the outside world. Marguerite in particular took charge of negotiations with the publishers, and it was she who handled the sums of money, which were not extraordinary but still relatively important, that were earned by the contracts for *My Life* and the *History*.

Jakob Frank (also known as Graef), a Lithuanian-Austrian who knew Russian, arrived on May 29 and served as a secretary till the end of October. Early July saw the arrival of Gérard Rosenthal and Pierre and Denise Naville, for discussions that were to lead to the formation in 1930 of a unified French Trotskyite group with Raymond Molinier, Pierre Frank, and Alfred Rosmer, and to the launching of a weekly in Paris, *La Vérité*. Robert Ranc, a Frenchman selected by Marguerite Rosmer, arrived at the beginning of October and stayed a few months as a secretary. Rosenthal returned at the end of January 1930 for about two months. And on April 15, 1930, Jan Frankel arrived from Prague, recommended as a secretary by Marguerite Rosmer. He was to stay much longer than anybody who had come before, and it was because of his presence in Prinkipo that Liova could leave for Berlin the next year.

Raymond and Jeanne Molinier continued to make periodic trips to Turkey, after one of which Raymond again returned alone to Paris, leaving Jeanne in Prinkipo. On a warm Turkish night, Jeanne and Liova became lovers. Jeanne saw the relationship only as a one-night affair and intended to go back to Paris to rejoin Raymond. Liova took the adventure much more seriously and even spoke of killing himself if Jeanne would not live with him. They stayed together, and with time, Jeanne became deeply attached to Liova. Her letters at the time of Liova's death in 1938 are full of heartrending despair. Trotsky became quite angry with Liova because of his liaison with Jeanne.

A few days after Liova's departure for Berlin, at two o'clock in the morning of March 1, 1931, the occupants of the villa Izzet Pasha were awakened by fire. Trotsky, Natalia, and Zina dashed into the garden. Frankel stayed in the burning house, throwing folders through the windows until the firemen, who had just arrived, forced him to leave. It was a flash fire, spreading rapidly and burning itself out. When I was in

Prinkipo, I saw books that had been charred on the outside but were otherwise undamaged. The fire had been caused by a water heater, installed in the attic, which had been left burning during the night. The fire affected only the attic and the second floor. The ground floor, where Zina and Frankel lived, remained untouched, and the house was left standing. The ceiling between the first and second floors did not even collapse. On the second floor itself, the fire, by moving so rapidly, had spared two closed closets, and their contents were found undamaged. Lost were books, a collection of photographs from the time of the Revolution, folders with clippings intended for a book on the world situation, personal belongings, and two Russian typewriters. Saved were the manuscript of the second volume of the *History,* on which Trotsky was then working, and the folders of correspondence with deportees in Siberia—in fact, all the important papers. When fleeing the house, Trotsky himself carried out the notebook containing the Siberian addresses.

In a conversation that I had with Natalia in 1958, she told me that only printed materials had been lost, except perhaps a few unanswered letters on Trotsky's desk or Maria Ilinishna's, as well as a few pages of an article that Trotsky was then writing on the Oustric affair in France. Several years afterward, Trotsky mentioned in a letter that a manuscript of his on Marx and Engels had been destroyed in the fire. Here I am inclined to think that his memory had failed him, for he contemplated working on this project at the start of 1933, long after the fire; he never mentioned this work in his letters of early 1931, and Natalia in her conversation with me in 1958 denied that such a manuscript had been lost in the fire.

The survivors of the fire went to the Savoy Hotel, where they settled in a detached building in the courtyard, which had three small rooms. Frankel stated later: "All of us felt dejected and were very much disturbed by the irreparable losses of the fire—all except Comrade Trotsky. No sooner were we settled than he laid out his manuscripts on the table, called over the stenographer, and began to dictate chapters of his book as though nothing at all had happened during the night." Trotsky later behaved in exactly the same way under similar circumstances after the first attempt on his life in Coyoacán, in the early morning of May 25, 1940. After being fired upon by the murderers, led by Siqueiros, and while awaiting the arrival of the Mexican police, Trotsky sat at his desk and started to write. Writing or dictating was his way of preserving his inner balance. A few days after the fire Raymond Molinier and his brother Henri arrived from Paris and started to look for a new dwelling, which they found in Moda.

When I arrived in Prinkipo, a political crisis in the French Trotskyite group had led to a break between Trotsky and the Rosmers, and their duties had been taken up by Raymond Molinier. The persons who then stood closest to Trotsky with respect to practical decisions were his son Liova in Berlin, Jan Frankel in Prinkipo, and Raymond Molinier in Paris. In certain matters Henri Molinier, too, played an important role. The climate in this entourage was markedly anti-Navillist. Liova and Frankel, to say nothing of the Molinier brothers, were much less subtle in their assessment of Naville than was Trotsky, who, although he had disagreements with Naville and was frequently angry with him, respected his intellectual qualities. At the top of a closet in our room Frankel kept two issues of *La Révolution surréaliste,* which he showed to newcomers as evidence of the excesses of Naville's surrealistic past.

Trotsky displayed all his amiability with visitors and newcomers. He would talk, explain, gesture, ask questions, and at times be really charming. The presence of a young woman seemed to give him special animation. But the more one worked with him, the more demanding and brusque he became. The situation in which we found ourselves had something to do with this change. We had to live together day in and day out, for months and soon years, in a restricted space, subject to constant security measures. Everything was arranged ahead, visits as well as outings. Nothing could be left to chance. "You treat me like an object," Trotsky once complained to me.

In the years from 1929 to 1940, Trotsky's third emigration, the three persons toward whom he allowed himself to be the most brusque were Liova, Jan Frankel, and me. Frankel told me that in Prinkipo the relations between Liova and his father had become so strained that at one time Liova talked of going to the Soviet consulate in Istanbul to find out about returning to Russia. Frankel never said that Liova actually took any steps in this direction; but in a letter from Liova to his mother, dated July 7, 1937, there are the strange words, "if I had been permitted to go back to the U.S.S.R. in 1929," which seem to indicate that Liova actually presented the Soviet consulate with a request to return and the request was denied. Trotsky lost all control when on February 15, 1937, because of a delay in the mailing of some depositions on the Moscow trials, he wrote to Liova, who was then living in Paris, "It is difficult for me to say whether the worst blows are falling on me from Moscow or from Paris."

As for my own relations with Trotsky, I felt a constant modulation in them. There were periods of cheerful and warm confidence, followed by moments, often without my understanding the reason for the change, of surliness and tension. Strangely enough, later on, in Mexico, Trotsky's relations with the American secretaries and guards were somehow simpler, perhaps more reserved, but also less variable. He was indeed older at that time, but possibly his impatience had also lost its cutting edge against the American placidity.

One of the incidents that showed his abruptness occurred in June 1933. After each fishing expedition we would take the outboard motor out of the boat and run it for a few minutes in a barrel of fresh water, to purge the cooling system of the sea water, which would corrode it. One day, after coming back from fishing in the morning, we realized that we had no more oil of the proper viscosity; all we had left was some oil of a different grade, used during the winter, and we had decided not to run the motor unless we had the proper oil. In the afternoon, I decided to clear the motor, because it was essential to discharge the sea water, even though it required a few minutes' use of the slightly different oil. So I started the motor in the barrel at the end of the garden near the wharf. As soon as Trotsky heard the stutter of the motor, he came out on the balcony of the house and shouted to me across the garden as loud as he could, "Stop that immediately!" At such moments it was useless to try to explain things to him.

With objects, Trotsky had limited and precise relations. There was in general a certain stiffness, a lack of naturalness and improvisation, in the way that he handled them. He had a number of possessions with which he felt at home: his pen, the outboard motor, the fishing gear, the hunting gun. These objects had to be handled according to certain rules, which could rarely be changed. For him to adapt himself to new equipment was always a complicated operation. His pen was of great importance to him, and the choice of a new one necessitated many trials. The fishing gear always took much of his attention. He prized the lines and hooks brought or sent to him from the United States. He operated the outboard motor according to the rules of the handbook and would tolerate no deviation. Frankel told me in Prinkipo that Trotsky, when still in Russia, had expressed the desire to have a car and to drive. Joffe, a Soviet diplomat and friend of Trotsky, sent him from abroad a Mercedes, specially equipped with a powerful engine. Trotsky took the wheel and, after five hundred yards, went into a ditch. That was the end of the driving. Later, during the summer of 1933 in Saint-Palais, when only Trotskyites were admitted to the house for reasons of security and we had no domestic help, the housework would fall on Jeanne Martin and Vera Lanis, Raymond Molinier's new companion, while the rest of us helped out as we could. In particular, there was the chore each evening of washing the dishes. One evening, Trotsky decided to give us a hand. He wiped each plate or glass with such extreme care that the operation went on late into the night, and everybody was much more tired than if he had not helped us.

Trotsky had no trinkets or souvenirs of any kind. For a time he kept near his bed a picture of Rakovsky, who had been perhaps his closest personal friend in Russia. The picture had been smuggled out of Russia in 1932. One day in April 1934, after Rakovsky's capitulation to Stalin, I was burning worthless papers, such as translation drafts, in the garden of the Barbizon villa. Trotsky came to me, gave me Rakovsky's picture, and said, "Here, you can burn that too."

The desk in his study was always loaded with papers. He would arrange them in his own manner, and he always knew where everything was. Nobody could touch the desk. Natalia would only dust it lightly. In Prinkipo, Trotsky had in his study a small steel box, which we called the treasury, in which he kept the most confidential letters. Later on, he kept nothing in his study, and everything went into the archives, classified by the secretaries. The only papers that were not stored in the folders of the archives were Sergei's letters, which Natalia kept in her room.

When I arrived in Prinkipo, there were staying in Istanbul an American, B. J. Field (whose real name was Gould), and his wife, Esther. Both had been members of the American Trotskyite group, from which they had been expelled during one of the factional fights. Field was an economist and had worked for a Wall Street firm. The world was then in the

Christian Rakovsky in Barnaul, Siberia,
1932—the photograph smuggled out to Trotsky.

depths of the depression. Trotsky, who was following the economic developments closely, valued Field's practical knowledge of economics. In the weeks after my arrival, a number of talks took place with Field. We would meet at half past four in Trotsky's study. The language used, if I remember correctly, was German. Trotsky even planned to write a book with Field on the world economic situation, but nothing ever came of the project. During these meetings, Esther Field sat in a corner and painted an oil portrait of Trotsky. I do not know what became of this portrait.

My departure for Prinkipo, first proposed for June 1932, had been postponed because of the possibility of a trip by Trotsky to Czechoslovakia in order to consult doctors and to spend time in a spa. During July

Trotsky near Marseilles on his way to Copenhagen, November 21, 1932.

and August there was continued uncertainty about Trotsky's trip; at times everything seemed arranged, then the plan was upset by the hesitations of the Czechoslovak government. In September it became clear that the trip could not take place, so my departure for Prinkipo was settled. When I arrived, a new plan was afoot, involving a trip by Trotsky to Copenhagen in order to deliver a lecture at the invitation of a Danish student organization. No arrangements had yet been made, but by the beginning of November matters had moved so quickly that there was no longer any time to settle numerous pending affairs before departure, and somebody had to stay behind. The lot fell on the one who had arrived last, namely me. Trotsky and the other occupants of the house, except Sieva and me, left Istanbul on November 14, 1932. Sieva was to go to Vienna, where his mother was on the point of moving from Berlin, but the Austrian consul in Istanbul had refused to grant a visa to the six-year-old boy without special instructions, which were late in coming. When they finally arrived, Sieva and I left Istanbul on November 23 for Marseilles. From there we took the train for Paris, where I stayed for about a week while Trotsky was in Copenhagen.

Trotsky had accepted the Danish students' invitation because it would give him an opportunity to defend his ideas through the spoken word and to meet a relatively large number of fellow-thinkers. About two dozen Trotskyites came to Copenhagen from various European countries and had political discussions with Trotsky. Perhaps he had also hoped that he would be allowed to settle in a Western European country. In any event, a request for a permanent visa, or at least a long residence permit, was discreetly presented to the Danish government, but to no avail. Since no other country offered to admit him, nothing was left but to go back to Prinkipo. The French government did not even allow Trotsky to stop over in Paris. Having arrived from Dunkirk on December 6 at the Gare du Nord at ten o'clock in the morning, he had to take the ten-past-eleven train for Marseilles from the Gare de Lyon.

The boat schedules were such that Trotsky would have to wait about ten days for the next boat to Istanbul. The French authorities had agreed that he could spend the time in a suburb of Marseilles, in a villa to be rented for the occasion. Henri Molinier had gone to Marseilles to look for a suitable place, and on December 4 I left Paris for Marseilles, where, together with Henri, I put the last touches to the arrangements in the villa that had been found. On December 6, I took the train for Avignon, to meet the train that was bringing Trotsky from Paris.

During the trip back to Marseilles, I shared a compartment with Trotsky and Liova. At one point I began to give them some information about the Trotskyite group in Paris, which I had been able to observe at close range during the preceding week. Trotsky stopped me, feeling sure, he said, that the French police had planted microphones in the railroad car. I tried to explain to him that it would be difficult at that time to use a microphone concealed in a moving train because of the background noise, but he remained skeptical.

The train made an unscheduled stop at a small station before Marseilles, Pas-des-Lanciers. We were supposed to meet Henri Molinier there with some cars for the drive to the villa. Henri was indeed there with the cars, but the plans had been changed. The French authorities had decided that we were to go directly to the harbor and board a small Italian ship, the *Campidoglio,* which was to sail for Istanbul the next day; at that point it was already late in the evening. This was a great disappointment, but nothing could be done. We set out for the harbor and located the *Campidoglio.* The boat turned out to be very small and very old, and was used, they told us, to transport plaster. The gangway was a mere plank, laid horizontally. Trotsky and Natalia went aboard with Raymond Molinier. I was still on the pier, taking care of some business, when Trotsky suddenly reappeared on the gangway and dashed down toward a police official who was standing on the pier. Natalia and Raymond followed close behind. Shaking his finger under the nose of the official, Trotsky shouted: "We cannot travel in such conditions. The French government has deceived us." It was one of the few times that I saw him in all his fury. "Do you believe that the French police have the right to put me by force on an Italian boat?" he shouted. The police official answered, "Yes," but did not have the audacity to prevent Trotsky physically from disembarking, although he had at his disposal all the power of the French state. It turned out that the freighter was indeed an old tub, which normally did not take passengers, and that arrangements had been made hastily, at the request of the French authorities, who wanted to get Trotsky out of their territory as quickly as possible. Besides the fact that the boat would take more than two weeks to reach Istanbul, it was scheduled to call at several ports for loading and unloading goods, which would produce a dreadful noise at all hours of the day and night.

There we stood on the pier, in the glare of floodlights, near the unfortunate *Campidoglio.* It was now midnight. Some of us sat on suitcases. Many policemen in uniform or in mufti stood around us; but there were no journalists, the French police having had no interest in making their actions known.

Discussions began. Telephone calls were made to Paris. On the pier, Trotsky dictated to me the text of a long telegram to be sent to Herriot, then Premier, and Chautemps and De Monzie, two of his ministers, in which he protested against the way the French police had deceived him. Somebody suggested that we might catch an Italian boat, a real passenger ship, bound for Istanbul, if Italy would grant us a transit visa. Since the *Campidoglio* would not be ready to weigh anchor until the next afternoon, the French police agreed that Trotsky and those with him could spend the rest of the night in a hotel in Marseilles, on the understanding that if in the morning Italy did not grant the visa, Trotsky would be put by force on the *Campidoglio*. At about half past three in the morning we settled into the Hotel Regina in Marseilles. Yet the day was not over for me. I had to remain on guard, sitting on a chair in the corridor by the door of the room where Trotsky and Natalia were sleeping.

The next day, December 7, Henri Molinier went to the Italian consulate. A telephone call was put through to Rome. The transit visa was granted. In the afternoon Trotsky, Natalia, Jan Frankel, Otto Schüssler, and I took the train for Ventimiglia. Trotsky and Natalia had to say goodbye to Liova, who was going back to Berlin. At the border an Italian police official was awaiting us. Relations between France and Italy were not good at the time, and after the Marseilles episode the Italian official could not restrain himself from taking a stab at France. "Here, Mr. Trotsky, you are free," he said. This was obviously an exaggeration, for we had to cross Italy on a prearranged schedule and under constant police surveillance. From Ventimiglia we went to Genoa, and from Genoa to Milan, where we arrived on December 8 in the morning. We left almost immediately for Venice, where we arrived shortly after three o'clock in the afternoon, intending to take the boat for Istanbul. Upon our arrival we learned that the boat had just left but that, if we took a train, we could catch the same boat in Brindisi, where it was scheduled to call. While waiting for the train, we visited the city with the police official and toured the canals in an official launch. At about nine o'clock in the evening we took the train for Brindisi, where the next day, on December 9, we immediately boarded the Italian steamship *Adria*.

During all these tribulations Trotsky was surly and uncommunicative. For the past few weeks he had been in contact again with people; now he had to give up western Europe and return to the isolation of Prinkipo. When the boat stopped at Piraeus, he did not go ashore. We arrived in Istanbul on December 11, late in the evening. We slept aboard and went to Prinkipo the next morning. Pierre Frank had come from Paris by train ahead of us and had determined that everything was in order in the house. Such was the end of the Copenhagen trip.

Life resumed as before in the Prinkipo house. Trotsky started to work again. He seemed to be full of renewed energy. Although he had been disappointed not to secure a residence permit in western Europe, he perhaps had never really believed that it was possible. His attention focused on two topics, the economic situation in Russia, which was then extremely critical, and the organizational strengthening of the international Trotskyite movement, which was beginning to make relative headway. On the subject of the Russian economy, I had a discussion with him about growth rates. With the help of a table of logarithms obtained at the French bookstore in Pera, I traced a number of curves based on various growth rates, which I gave to him. He put the sheets on his desk, but never used them. I got the impression that he mistrusted a mathematical argument that was not immediately transparent to him.

On Christmas Eve there was a huge storm. The sea was so wild that even in the small inner basin at the house pier the two fishing boats were unsafe. Waves swept over the pier. In the dark of night we had to lift the boats from the water by sheer physical strength and carry them into the garden. Trotsky assisted us, full of vigor.

When Trotsky had left the Soviet consulate in Istanbul in 1929, after his brief residence there, the Soviet government had given him a sum of fifteen hundred dollars as "royalties." Trotsky had also received at that time a Soviet passport, in which his profession was listed as "writer." Paid interviews for the world press subsequently earned Trotsky a modest amount of money, which was used for the living expenses in Turkey. Contracts for his books, above all for *My Life* and the *History,* brought in larger sums. Part of this money was used to finance the publication of the *Bulletin of the Opposition* and also to launch a number of Trotskyite newspapers, like *La Vérité.* Small sums of money were sent to deportees in Siberia.

In the midst of the poverty that was then the lot of all revolutionaries, Trotsky's contracts with publishers thus provided him with relative affluence. But by the time of my arrival in Prinkipo in October 1932, this affluence was coming to an end. The Copenhagen trip, involving travel expenses for a large number of persons, caused a substantial financial loss, in spite of the money paid to Trotsky for the trip by the Danish organizers and the American broadcasting companies. In the following months the financial difficulties mounted.

Jan Frankel left Prinkipo on January 5, 1933, in order to work in Paris
at the International Secretariat, which was being transferred there from
Berlin. On the same day Zina killed herself by inhaling gas in Berlin.
She was found dead at two o'clock in the afternoon. Liova sent Natalia a
telegram, which arrived on January 6, just as we were finishing lunch. If
I remember correctly, Pierre Frank was on guard duty and gave the
telegram to Natalia as she was going back to the second floor. Trotsky
and Natalia immediately shut themselves in their room, without telling
us anything. We felt that something grave had happened, but did not
know what. We learned the news from the afternoon newspapers. During the days that followed, Trotsky at times half-opened the door of
their room to ask for tea. When a few days later he came out to resume
work in his study, his features appeared ravaged. Two deep wrinkles
had formed on either side of his nose and ran down both sides of his
mouth. His first task was to dictate a public letter to the Central Committee of the Russian Communist party, in which he placed the responsibility for his daughter's death upon Stalin.

I never met Zina. Jan Frankel and Jeanne Martin spoke to me about
her. Of Trotsky's four children, she was the one most similar to her
father physically and, in a way, also morally. The letters that she wrote
to her father were full of passion. When she and her son Sieva came out
of Russia at the end of 1930, they were the last members of Trotsky's
family to leave Russia. The child's father, Platon Volkov, had been deported to Siberia. Zina and Sieva spent only nine months together in
Turkey before she left alone for Berlin, where she was to meet Liova and
Jeanne Martin and intended to undertake psychoanalysis. Trotsky was
angry at her for leaving Sieva in Prinkipo. On June 30, 1932, he wrote to
Liova: "Mama [Natalia] is tied down both hands and feet by Sieva . . .
We must settle the question of Sieva as fast as possible." The last sentence refers to Sieva's prospective departure for Germany to be with his
mother. When I arrived in Prinkipo in October 1932, Sieva was still
there. He was a gentle, quiet little boy, who went to school in the morning and made himself scarce in the house. Natalia was far from being
"tied hands and feet" by him.

In Berlin, Zina found a Jewish doctor who spoke Russian fluently,
with whom she began treatment. Jeanne saw her frequently. Sieva, having traveled with me from Prinkipo to Paris, left Paris on December 14,

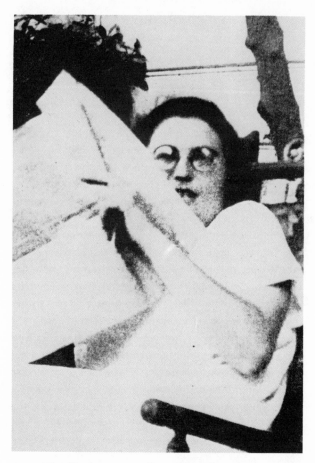

Zinaida Lvovna Volkova in Moda, 1931.

for Berlin, where he was reunited with his mother after more than a year.

Years later, in a letter dated March 27, 1959, Jeanne wrote to me about Trotsky's daughter: "Zina had, in short, somewhat forgotten Platon. Since they had been separated for so long, one could hardly reproach her for that. She was on the way to recovery from tuberculosis. She absolutely did not want to return to Russia, quite the contrary. It was L.D. who wanted her to consider going back, for she had begun to behave not very reasonably from several points of view. She dreaded nothing more than to find herself one day forced to return to Russia. She actually had been delirious at times and had been treated for that in a clinic, but she never lost her mind completely, and the attacks never lasted long. The doctor, whom we questioned about what to do with Sieva, advised us to leave him with her, perhaps for her own good; he did not see any danger for Sieva. At the fatal moment, you know, she had the foresight to put him far from her. Her last thought was for him. She had, of course, many complexes, which seems quite natural, if that is the word, in view of her life before her arrival in Berlin. But I do not think that she was driven to kill herself by the thought of the imminent return of her mental illness, from which she seemed to have been cured, because she had freely left the clinic and gone back to live with Sieva in her boardinghouse. She was *desperate,* but of her despair I can only *speak* with you; I cannot *write* about it. Her despair was spread out in the papers that she left in her apartment, without trying to destroy them, not even thinking of that. I ask myself why we did not destroy all of them, but it was not for me to take the initiative. And if Leon [Liova] thought it well to keep them . . . Anyhow, they were seized by the police during two searches of my apartment [in Paris] after Leon's death, and it is dreadful to think that the police put their dirty hands on these things that were so delicate and painful. It was never possible to recover them, even to trace them, after the war when we tried officially to claim them, together with the papers that had been seized in our apartment. They had all disappeared, we were finally told."

In a conversation that I had with Jeanne in September 1959, she mentioned three other facts. First, when Zina was in Berlin, she did not confide in Liova. Before killing herself, it was to Jeanne that she left a short letter. In that perfectly lucid note she wrote: "Take good care of Sieva, he is sweet." Second, at the time of her death Zina was pregnant, a point on which Jeanne made no further comment. Third, during Zina's treatment, Trotsky sent to her analyst the letters that he had received from her. He undoubtedly thought that he was thus helping the doctor, but Zina learned about it and was deeply wounded. Zina's last letters to her father show that she felt abandoned. On December 14, 1932, she wrote to him, "Dear papa, I expect a letter from you, if only a few lines."

The personal tragedy that the death of his daughter meant for Trotsky merged with the political tragedy that was falling over Europe. On January 30, 1933, Hindenburg asked Hitler to become Chancellor of the Reich. Germany then found itself in an ambiguous situation. The two large working-class parties and the trade unions remained intact, while the reins of government were held by the Nazi party. On March 2, during one of our afternoon discussions in Trotsky's study, he told us about the situation in Germany: "We must take full advantage of all possibilities. It is as if you must climb a steep mountain, which you think is just a smooth wall; when you are in front of it, it seems impossible for you to climb. But if you take advantage of every crevice, of every natural step, of every hole, in order to hold on with your hands and grip with your feet, then you can climb the highest rock under the most difficult conditions. For that, you must have courage, but also foresight and perspicacity." Yet the working-class organizations did nothing, and Hitler grew bolder. The Reichstag fire, engineered by the Nazis themselves on February 27, allowed him to sweep away the trade unions and working-class parties, and on March 5 Hitler established his totalitarian regime.

Trotsky's reaction came quickly. On March 14, he finished an article entitled "The Tragedy of the German Proletariat," bearing the subtitle "The German Workers Will Rise Again; Stalinism — Never!" Until then Trotsky's policy had been the reform of the official Communist organizations, and the day-to-day activities of Trotskyite groups had been directed entirely to trying to be heard by members of the official Communist organizations. The Trotskyite opposition considered itself as belonging to the Third International, even though it had been formally expelled. Here and there on the fringe of the Trotskyite organization, individuals or small groups had advocated the formation of a new International, but Trotsky had resolutely rejected the idea. Thus, to abandon the policy of reform represented a sharp break with the past. The change in policy went through several stages.

As early as his conversation of March 2, Trotsky had told us: "I am certain that, if Hitler remains at the helm in Germany and the [Communist] party collapses, then a new party will have to be built. But the most important constituent of the new party will be recruited from the old party." Yet this view still related to a hypothetical situation. After the catastrophe of March 5, Trotsky in the March 14 article rejected as out-of-date the policy of reforming the German Communist party, but he clung to the policy of reform for the other parties of the Communist International, in particular for the Russian party. However, the problem of the International as a whole could not fail to be raised. In April the Executive Committee of the Communist International unanimously adopted a resolution proclaiming that the policy of noncooperation with the Socialists followed by the German Communist party "had been entirely correct up to and including the time of the Hitler coup d'état." The Executive Committee, on Stalin's orders, was supporting Stalin. There were isolated reactions, here and there, in the ranks of the Communist parties; but as an organization, the Communist International was in Stalin's grip. The policy of reform was losing all reality.

In Trotsky's gradual renunciation of the reform policy, the Russian party posed a particular problem. Some time after the April resolution of the Communist International, Trotsky told us in Prinkipo: "Since April we have been for reform in every country except Germany, where we have been for a new party. We can now take a symmetrical position, that is, to be for a new party in every country except the U.S.S.R., where we shall be for the reform of the Bolshevik party." This position was never stated in writing, except perhaps in a letter to Liova; but I am not even sure of that. In any case, the position was quickly abandoned. On July 15, 1933, Trotsky, under the pseudonym of G. Gurov, sent to the Trotskyite groups an article entitled "It Is Necessary To Build Anew Communist Parties and a Communist International." In that article the policy of reform was abandoned with respect to all Communist organizations dominated by Stalin. This policy, explained the article, had now become "utopian and reactionary."

The political turn coincided by chance with a change of residence. Trotsky left Turkey on July 17 to settle in France. When he landed in France on July 24, the translations of the July article had barely reached the hands of the leaders of the various Trotskyite groups. During the following weeks, which were the first spent by Trotsky in France, the new policy provoked lively discussion.

It was also in the spring of 1933 that communications with Russia ceased altogether. When the leaders of the Trotskyite opposition had been deported to Siberia at the end of 1927 and the beginning of 1928, they were at first able to correspond rather freely among themselves. Because they had occupied important positions in the government of the country, having had political, economic, or diplomatic posts, the correspondence exchanged between the various places of deportation in Siberia contains rich material on the political and economic problems of the time. Certain letters are in fact small treatises on Marxist theory. In the second half of 1928, although censorship became harsher, the deportees could still communicate among themselves, most often by postcard or telegram. When Trotsky was living in Alma-Ata, as Natalia later told me, communications were still possible between him and the opposition group left in Moscow. When a flower pot would appear at a certain window, this was the sign that a courier had arrived from Moscow. Liova had charge of these contacts.

After his arrival in Turkey in 1929, Trotsky still had relations by mail with perhaps twenty Siberian deportees. They did not write to Prinkipo but to various addresses in France and Germany. Most often, they wrote only a postcard, containing little more than personal news. With the passing years, communications became rarer and rarer, although in 1932, news still filtered through. It was at this time that Rakovsky's photograph came out of Russia. Liova was in charge of all these contacts as well, first in Prinkipo and then in Berlin. From time to time a small sum of money was sent to a deportee. Communications with persons in Moscow or Leningrad had by then ceased. The only exception was Zina's mother, Alexandra Lvovna Bronstein, who was living in Leningrad and with whom Zina corresponded. When Zina died, Trotsky received a letter from her mother, which he answered. He wrote his letter by hand and gave me the sealed envelope, on which he had himself inscribed the address in his fine handwriting. He asked me to send the letter registered, with a return receipt requested. The return receipt never came back. This was the time, in the first months of 1933, that communications with Russia ceased completely. Not until several years later did direct news come from Russia with the escapees Tarov, Ciliga, Victor Serge, Reiss, and Krivitsky. But by that time, relations with the opposition groups in Siberia had long since terminated.

In May 1933 we learned through the newspapers that Maxim Gorky, on his way back from Italy to Russia aboard a Soviet ship, the *Jean Jaurès,* would pass through Istanbul. Trotsky told Pierre Frank and me to try to see Gorky, in order to obtain information about the Trotskyite exiles in Siberia. On the day announced by newspapers, we found the *Jean Jaurès* berthed at a quay in Istanbul and we went on board. We were asked who we were and what we wanted. "We are French Communists and we want to see Gorky." Four or five solidly built fellows immediately positioned themselves around us. But soon Peshkov, Gorky's adopted son, arrived. We told him exactly who we were. He showed no hostility toward us. His adoptive father, he told us, could not receive us because of ill health, and he asked us what he could do instead. We told him that we had recently received alarming news from Russia about Rakovsky's situation. Throughout this conversation, one or two guardian spirits were cocking their ears, trying to follow the words. Peshkov promised us that he would speak to Gorky, and we left the boat. But no news ever came from that direction.

The first six months of 1933 saw a great physical change in Trotsky. The two furrows that had appeared on his face after Zina's death did not disappear and, with time, grew deeper. When I had arrived in Prinkipo in the previous October, Trotsky was definitely turning gray, although here and there he still had black in his hair. His face and head were still remarkably similar to their appearance in photographs of 1924 or 1925. But in the first six months of 1933, his hair turned considerably grayer. Often, instead of wearing it proudly brushed back, he combed it to the side. In a few months, almost a few weeks, his features became what they would remain till his death. Those who knew Trotsky personally have often noted how carefully he dressed. When I myself first met him, he was immaculately garbed in white. But in the spring of 1933, he began to show less care about his clothing.

The season had something to do with Trotsky's depressed condition. February was quite cold, with icy winds blowing from the Black Sea. The house had no heating, except for charcoal braziers. Because of the wind, fishing was impossible for days on end. One afternoon, after we had been unable to fish for more than a week, Natalia, Frank, and I had a talk. We were upset by the fact that Trotsky had no physical activity, and I was chosen to ask him whether he would like to go rabbit shooting on the Little Island, Küchük Ada, an uninhabited islet southwest of Prinkipo. I knocked on the door of his study. "Da!" he answered. I went in and explained the plan to him. "Pooh! To shoot rabbits!" he said with a wry face. He obviously could stir up no interest in the project.

Little by little the long fishing expeditions of the morning were abandoned. Now we would leave at half past four in the afternoon, after his rest, and did not go far. Often we stayed within sight of the house. We made a few trials and, if they were not successful, Trotsky shrugged his shoulders, saying "Niet rybi [No fish]!" and we went back.

It was during one of these short afternoon fishing expeditions that we almost met our death. It must have been May. Trotsky, Kharalambos, and I had left at about half past four. We were not planning to go far and did not even take a Turkish policeman with us, which was unusual and probably saved our lives. The sky was gray, but since the weather seemed calm, Kharalambos had agreed to the trip.

Though no longer within sight of the house, we were still not far off, somewhere between Prinkipo and Halki, when a north wind sprang up. In a few minutes, it was a storm. Kharalambos, who immediately perceived the danger, stopped the motor. He asked us to stretch out in the bottom of the boat so as to lower the center of gravity, and he began to row with a single oar. There we were, Trotsky and I, lying in the bottom of the boat, half covered with water. After each wave, the boat fell back in the trough with a thud. Kharalambos handled the oar with one hand, while with the other he bailed out. This lasted perhaps half an hour. Driven by the wind and somewhat guided by Kharalambos, the boat was carried little by little to the southern side of the island, where we found calmer waters and could get ashore. We made a fire to dry off. Trotsky and I then walked back to the house, while Kharalambos waited with the boat for better weather. Meanwhile Natalia, who from the house had seen the danger, had taken a horse carriage, with Pierre Frank, to try to find us. But in the western part of the island, off which we were located, the road swerves from the coast and wanders through a pine forest; thus Frank and she could not see us.

In their personal remembrances Pierre Naville and Gérard Rosenthal have both noted Trotsky's use of the verb "to shoot" in conversation during 1929 and 1930. After I arrived in Prinkipo, I heard him say more than once about adversaries who were annoying him, "You know, they should be shot." After the spring of 1933 the word vanished from his vocabulary. He would no longer allow himself this kind of irony.

It was also at this time that our financial difficulties grew worse. After Hitler's rise to power, royalties stopped coming from Germany. The money accruing from royalties in the United States, which was deposited in a bank in New York and formed the best part of our income, lost much of its value when Roosevelt devaluated the dollar in April 1933. After Trotsky came back from Copenhagen at the end of 1932, he had no big book in progress. He thought for a while of writing a study of the world economic and political situation; then an account of the relations between Marx and Engels, to be called "The Romance of a Great Friendship"; then a history of the Red Army; then a series of portraits of Soviet diplomats, such as Rakovsky, Ioffe, Vorovsky, and Krasin. But all these projects remained only plans. No contract was signed, and so no royalties were received. Paid articles written for the world press also became rarer, both because Trotsky was engrossed with the turn toward the new International and because the editors of newspapers and magazines had seen their funds reduced. On April 27, 1933, I wrote to Liova that all we had left was $1,780, and that there was no prospect of getting any income in the near future. Natalia and I would go over the accounts, trying to cut expenses wherever possible. An American, Sara Jacobs, who knew Russian and was a member of the American Trotskyite organization, offered to come to Prinkipo and work without pay as a typist. The offer was accepted, since it would save Maria Ilinishna's salary. Sara arrived in June, and on June 18 Maria Ilinishna stopped working.

After the return from Copenhagen, there had been continual comings and goings. Jan Frankel left in January, and Arne Swabeck arrived in February, to stay a few weeks. On April 10, Otto Schüssler left for Prague, where he was to work on the publication of the new German Trotskyite paper for the émigrés, *Unser Wort* ("Our Word"). His replacement as German secretary in Prinkipo was Rudolf Klement, a young student from Hamburg, who arrived on April 27. Max Shachtman, one of the leaders of the American Trotskyite organization, arrived on May 23 and left Turkey with us in July when we went to France. Pierre Frank left Prinkipo on June 22 to go back to Paris. Erwin Ackerknecht, then the foremost leader of the German Trotskyite group, arrived on July 7, but his stay was cut short because we were to leave for France a few days later. Each new arrival, which took place every two or three months, was always an event in the life of the household.

In 1933, malaria was still prevalent in Prinkipo, and all of us in the house were taking quinine, which made us a bit deaf. In spite of the quinine, in May I had more and more frequent attacks of fever, until it became necessary to consider my entering the French hospital in Istanbul. The chief doctor at the hospital, a Frenchman, was Professor Gassin. During the few weeks in 1929 when Trotsky had lived at the Soviet consulate in Istanbul, Minsky, the chief G.P.U. agent there, had given

Trotsky, Arne Swabeck, and Pierre Frank (standing),
Jean van Heijenoort and Rudolf Klement (seated),
in the garden at Prinkipo, May 1933.

him information about the secret agents of the big powers in Turkey. He had told him, in particular, that Dr. Gassin was one of the chiefs of French espionage in that part of the world. Trotsky or somebody else in the house had, I believe, later medically consulted the doctor. On May 25, the day of my departure for the hospital, while I was in bed with fever, Trotsky came to see me in my room. He told me about Dr. Gassin's activities, then said: "Oh, you know, the hospital is not bad. It is almost as good as jail; one can read there in peace." I spent about ten days in the hospital.

At the beginning of June, the French writer Georges Simenon, who was passing through Istanbul, sent Trotsky a letter, asking him for an interview for *Paris-Soir*. Trotsky received him on June 6 and gave him a long statement, which was published. Trotsky's most significant remark was: "Fascism, and especially German national-socialism, are bringing to Europe an undeniable danger of war. Being an outsider, I may be mistaken, but it seems to me that the extent of the danger is not sufficiently realized. If one has in view a perspective not of months but of years, though certainly not of tens of years, I consider it absolutely inevitable for fascist Germany to erupt in war. This is precisely the question that can decide Europe's fate." These words may seem banal today, because history has confirmed them so exactly. But if we turn to what politicians and journalists were saying at that time, when there were still so many illusions about the Führer's role, their prophetic force shines through. During the conversation, Simenon asked Trotsky if he was ready to "serve again" in Russia in case of danger, to which Trotsky nodded affirmatively. Simenon gave Trotsky one of his novels, in which the action takes place in Africa. Trotsky read the book and spoke highly of it to us, having found that the exploitation of blacks was quite well described.

After the formation of the Daladier government, Maurice Parijanine undertook to start a campaign to allow Trotsky to live in France. He approached a number of representatives and politicians, pursuing his efforts with vigor and skill. Trotsky had given his consent and even written a few letters that Parijanine had asked him for, although Trotsky displayed little hope. He was still under the expulsion order issued against him by the French government in 1916. Much had changed since then, but administrative decrees remain. On July 4 Parijanine wrote to Trot-

*Jean van Heijenoort and Max Shachtman in Istanbul,
July 12, 1933, just after van Heijenoort had left
the French consulate, carrying in his briefcase
Trotsky's and Natalia's passports stamped with their visas.*

Jan Frankel, Jean van Heijenoort, and Max Shachtman
in the garden at Prinkipo on the morning of
the final departure from Turkey, July 17, 1933.

sky that the expulsion order had been rescinded. In Prinkipo, this eli-
cited surprise. On July 12, I went to the French consulate in Istanbul to
have the French visa stamped in Trotsky's and Natalia's passports.
Everything went smoothly. The visas were granted without explicit restrictions.

We now had to organize the move. It would not be a round trip this
time, as when Trotsky had left for Copenhagen. Archives and books had
to be carried with us, packed in large wooden crates. On July 15, Jan
Frankel arrived from Paris. He was to stay on after our departure to settle the question of the house with the landlord and to sell the boats and
other belongings. On July 17 Trotsky, Natalia, Max Shachtman, Sara
Jacobs, Rudolf Klement, and I left for Marseilles on the Italian ship
Bulgaria. A barge had drawn up to the house pier to load the crates and
transport them directly to the ship. At the last moment a launch arrived
to take us to the ship, which weighed anchor late in the afternoon. By
sunset we were on the Sea of Marmara, and from the deck Trotsky
watched Istanbul vanish over the horizon.

2. FRANCE

When the boat called at Piraeus, Trotsky and Natalia stayed aboard. At Catania, Natalia went ashore with me, and perhaps also at Naples, but Trotsky never once left the ship. He was suffering from lumbago. He spent, in effect, the whole trip in his cabin, most of the time lying down. He wrote a short article on Ignazio Silone's book *Fontamara*. The article's dateline, "Aboard the *Bulgaria,* July 19, 1933," shows a touch of irony, since the book is an attack upon Fascism and we were aboard an Italian ship.

On July 24 in the morning, as we were getting close to Marseilles, the ship's captain told us that he had received radio instructions for the boat to stop at a certain place off Marseilles and wait for a launch. Thinking that we were all meant to take the launch, we got ourselves ready. Suddenly the launch appeared and drew alongside the ship. The only person to come aboard was Liova. He gave me a letter containing instructions on what I was to do and then quickly got into the launch with his father and mother, taking only a few handbags, and the launch disappeared. Our ship got under way again toward Marseilles. Everything had happened so fast that we had kept our guns, which later caused me difficulties with the French customs since we disembarked as ordinary passengers.

Liova's instructions were that I was to go from Marseilles to Lyons by train, with a few suitcases; from Lyons, after making sure that no journalist was on my track, I was to cross France and to meet Liova at the Saintes railway station, near the Atlantic coast, two days later at a certain time in the morning. All the other members of our group were to go to Paris by train, with the bulk of the luggage, and stay there awaiting further instructions. All these plans were designed to throw journalists and, if possible, the G.P.U. off the scent. Accordingly, on the morning of July 26, I met Liova at the Saintes railroad station, and we were soon in the villa where Trotsky had already settled down. It was near the small

*Trotsky and Liova in front of the Sea Spray villa
in Saint-Palais, August 1933.*

town of Saint-Palais, perhaps eight miles north of Royan. The villa was near the sea, at a spot where the coast is rocky and forms a bluff, about one mile north of the center of Saint-Palais, close to a beach called the Grande Côte. The villa, called Les Embruns ("Sea Spray"), was surrounded by a large garden, and there were no immediate neighbors. It had been found by Raymond Molinier, who had chosen well. Moreover, as it was summertime, the whole coast was full of vacationists, so that in the weeks to follow nobody would pay any particular attention to the occupants of the villa, even if their way of life was slightly out of the ordinary.

I was told the story of the trip from Marseilles to Saint-Palais. The launch had landed in Cassis, where an official of the Sûreté Générale had made Trotsky countersign a paper giving him permission to reside in France, subject to the same restrictions as any other alien, without special conditions. From Cassis, the travelers had gone by car through Aix-en-Provence, Montpellier, Albi, and Montauban. After spending the night in Tonneins, a small town in Aquitaine, they had arrived in Saint-Palais on July 25 in the afternoon. A brush fire occurring near the house at the very moment of their arrival had somewhat delayed their moving in. What with the firemen and the crowd of onlookers, there had even been some fear that Trotsky would be recognized. But nothing happened. He stayed in the car, holding a handkerchief over the lower part of his face as if he had a cold, until he could finally enter the house. The trip, all in all, had gone well. The only trouble spot had been Trotsky's health; because he was still suffering from lumbago, each bump during the car trip had been painful.

Meanwhile the press published the news that Trotsky had gone to Royat, a small resort town near Clermont-Ferrand, some two hundred miles from Royan. I never learned how this false information originated. Had there been a leak, followed by a one-letter distortion of the name? Had the French police, as a trick, given some friendly journalist a name that was similar? During our stay in Saint-Palais we had many visitors. Nevertheless, the secret of the Sea Spray villa remained well guarded.

Soon after our arrival, I went to La Rochelle to see the prefect of the department, who had been notified of Trotsky's coming. The details of Trotsky's sojourn had been arranged in Paris between high officials of the Sûreté Générale and Henri Molinier. I gave the prefect our exact location, and he assured me that nobody else in the department would learn of it. As the conversation took a somewhat less official turn, he told me that he had known Rakovsky in Montpellier when they both were students.

I also paid a visit to the landlord, who lived a few miles away. He was a collector, and told me more than I cared to know about Henri IV fireplaces. During our stay in his villa he never came there, and he never learned, at least not till much later, who had lived in his house.

On August 3 Rudolf Klement arrived from Paris to resume his work as German secretary. Sara Jacobs, the Russian typist, also came soon. Typewriters started to bang away in the house. No person alien to our group entered the house. Jeanne Martin and Vera Lanis were in charge of cooking and housekeeping. Vera, who had been born in Bessarabia and spoke Russian, was by then the companion of Raymond Molinier. Young Trotskyites from Paris came to help us with the guard. As in Prinkipo, somebody was on duty through the night making the rounds.

During our stay in Saint-Palais, Trotsky left the villa only for rare, brief automobile outings in late afternoon, through countryside which was covered with vineyards. Raymond Molinier brought from Paris two German shepherds, Benno and Stella, male and female, with whom Trotsky often played, throwing sticks for them to retrieve.

At the beginning of August, Raymond brought André Malraux from Paris by car. It must have been within a day or so of August 7. The travelers arrived in the evening, and after a conversation with Trotsky, Malraux went to spend the night in a hotel in Saint-Palais or Royan. The next morning he came back to the house. On that day Malraux and Trotsky had long talks alone in the study; Malraux later published an account of these talks. The conversations ran upon art in Russia after the Revolution, the problem of individualism and communism, the causes of the Red Army's defeat in Poland in 1920, and the strategy of a future war between Japan and Russia. There were also conversations in the garden, in which the whole household took part. During the previous spring, in Prinkipo, Trotsky had read Céline's *Voyage au bout de la nuit* and had written an article about the book. Trotsky and Malraux talked of Céline, Trotsky standing on the steps of the house, Malraux lower, at the foot of the steps. Malraux, who knew Céline, began to mimic him, imitating his gestures and way of speaking.

*Rudolf Klement, Trotsky, Yvan Craipeau, Jeanne Martin,
Sara Jacobs, and (seated on the floor) Jean van Heijenoort
in Saint-Palais, August 1933.*

*Trotsky with Benno and Stella behind the villa
in Saint-Palais, August 1933.*

If I remember correctly, Malraux did not take any meals with us. In the evening, before parting, Trotsky and Malraux went for a walk in the countryside, on which I accompanied them. Soon we came to the top of a cliff overlooking the ocean. The sun had just set. Malraux's nervous, jerky gestures stood out against the darkening sky, while Trotsky maintained the precise, controlled, didactic gestures of one who explains. At the foot of the cliff, the sea was breaking against the rocks. The last topic of conversation was death. "There is one thing that communism will never conquer, and that is death," Malraux said in substance. Trotsky answered him back, "When a man has done the tasks that he has set himself, when he has done what he wanted to do, death is simple."

After Malraux's departure, Trotsky made no reference to him that I can remember. In those days, we were preoccupied with politics and organizational matters. Trotsky had set his course toward a new International, which was a change in the orientation of the Trotskyite movement. On July 27, shortly after our arrival in Saint-Palais, all the occupants of the house met for a discussion of the new goal. Some remarks made by Trotsky during that conversation reveal the political climate of those days: "There is the secondary and subordinate question of a name. Fourth International? It is not very pleasant. When we broke with the Second International, we changed our theoretical foundations. Now, no; we remain based on the first four congresses [of the Communist International]. We could also proclaim: the Communist International is us! And call ourselves the Communist International (Bolsheviks-Leninists). There are pros and cons. The title of Fourth International is neater. This may be an advantage as far as large masses are concerned. For the slower selection of cadres, there is probably some advantage on the other side, in being called the Communist International (Bolsheviks-Leninists)." The ultimate hesitation expressed in these words was the last of the stages through which Trotsky went in passing from the policy of reform to that of a new International. But his doubts did not last long. Although the new organization was to stay far from the "large masses" and to concern itself with "the slower selection of cadres," he soon adopted the name of Fourth International.

The new orientation was quickly accepted by Trotskyites all over the world. The policy of reform had indeed exhausted all its possibilities. But beyond this acceptance, there suddenly arose the added problem of establishing relations with a number of independent groups. Hitler's rise to power, the paralysis of the large working-class organizations, the cretinism of the German Stalinists — all these had shaken certain people. Throughout western Europe, socialist and communist groups that had long been independent of the two large Internationals or had recently been severed from one of them were looking for new paths. The Independent Labour party in England, Sneevliet's and de Kadt's parties in Holland, the S.A.P. in the German emigration, and several other organizations here and there were ready to lend an ear to the Trotskyite views. Trotsky himself was no longer thousands of miles away in Prinkipo; he was now in France, able and willing to meet and talk with the leaders of these groups. The visitors would come to Paris, whence Raymond Molinier would take them by car — two, three, or four at a time — to Saint-Palais. Or Liova would give them confidential travel instructions in Paris and I would meet them at the Saintes railroad station.

Trotsky's meeting with Sneevliet was particularly cordial. They had known each other in Moscow and had met again in Copenhagen in November 1932. They spoke German together, using the familiar second person singular, as can be done in German, Russian, or French. Trotsky used this form with no other non-Russian and, among the Russians, only with Rakovsky, as far as I know.

It was during Trotsky's stay in Saint-Palais that the first crack occurred in his relations with Raymond Molinier, in whom he had placed so much confidence. During the various political discussions and negotiations of August 1933, Trotsky had the opportunity to observe Molinier's way of doing things much better than in the somewhat artificial conditions of Prinkipo. At the end of almost every afternoon in late August Trotsky dictated a short note to me, which in the evening I took to Royan and read to Raymond Molinier over the telephone. These notes were then destroyed. At the time a factional fight was taking place inside the French Trotskyite group. The leadership of the Trotskyites, in which Molinier then played the chief role, was opposed by the "Jewish group," a faction composed of fur workers from the Paris Jewish district, plus a few students. In October 1933 there would be a split, and an opposition faction would form a new group, called the Unified Communist Union; but in August, we had not yet reached that stage. Molinier was impatient with the opposition and wanted to provoke its expulsion as quickly as possible. Trotsky's notes to Molinier generally stressed the need to pursue the struggle on the plane of political discussion, to answer the opposition's arguments, and to clarify differences, but not to hasten organizational measures leading to a split.

In Saint-Palais, Trotsky could not fail to detect from his contact with numerous visitors that Raymond Molinier's financial undertakings had also generated hostility and suspicion. Raymond and Henri Molinier were "in business." They would buy outstanding bills at a fraction of their nominal value and then try to collect the money by methods that, though perhaps not transgressing the law, included threats and blackmail. Their company was called the French Collection Institute, and its methods had become notorious throughout the business world of Paris. In the spring of 1936, for instance, when it became necessary for me to look for work and I answered a newspaper ad, my prospective employer asked me for references. Obviously I could not give the name of Trotsky. Taken unawares, I answered that I had worked for Raymond Molinier. When he heard the name, the man's face filled with terror and he shouted, "Out!" By shady means, Raymond and Henri Molinier were acquiring sums of money that, though perhaps not enormous, seemed considerable in view of the state of destitution in which most Trotskyite militants then lived.

In September, Natalia left Saint-Palais for Paris, to stay there a few weeks visiting friends. It was the first time since they had left Moscow in 1927 that Trotsky and she were separated. In Saint-Palais, the stream of visitors was ebbing. The lines of political demarcation were now being drawn. It was becoming clear that, after a period of curiosity and even friendly interest, quite a number of groups wanted to keep their distance from Trotskyism. The British Independent Labour party and the German S.A.P. were not to become part of the Trotskyite movement.

In the first days of September Trotsky had long conversations with Fritz Sternberg, a German economist who Trotsky hoped could be persuaded to write the section on the world economic situation in the program of the new International. But nothing came of this idea, because Sternberg drifted away from Trotskyism. Incidentally, the only persons with whom Trotsky ever contemplated a literary collaboration were economists: Field in Prinkipo, Sternberg in Saint-Palais, and Otto Rühle in Mexico. This coincidence perhaps betrays a lack of confidence on Trotsky's part in his command of economics.

On September 10 a French Trotskyite, Louis Saufrignon from Poitiers, came to visit Trotsky. The talk turned on the new course of establishing the Fourth International. "In short," Saufrignon asked Trotsky, "what you are proposing is to begin all over again?" "Exactly," answered Trotsky. At the end of the conversation when everybody was getting up, Saufrignon asked Trotsky point blank, "Comrade Trotsky, what do you think of Stalin?" which was indeed a visitor's question. Trotsky's answer, in its entirety, was, "He is a man of prodigious will."

In Saint-Palais Trotsky's health began to improve and he suffered less from lumbago. During the first three weeks of August, which were filled with visits and talks, he actually felt quite well. But at the end of August he was seized by a high fever, the same one that had stricken him at different times in his life and which doctors, to hide their ignorance behind a Greek word, used to call a "cryptogenic" fever. During the following weeks his illness had ups and downs.

In mid-September the weather changed. The sunny days of summer vanished, and winds and storms raged over the Atlantic Ocean. The villa deserved its name, Sea Spray. The sea beat at the foot of the rocky cliff that ran beside the garden. Trotsky, not feeling well, stayed in bed for whole days. I would bring him the newspapers. His features became drawn and his hair disheveled. But if there were bad days, there were also much better ones, during which he wrote and received visitors.

During Trotsky's stay in the Sea Spray villa some forty-five visitors, many of them foreigners, came to see him for political discussions. In Paris, Henri Molinier received no complaints from the Sûreté Générale about these visits, which seems to indicate, as the prefect of Charente-Inférieure had assured me, that the police were not watching the villa. For our part, we conducted our own surveillance of the surrounding countryside. Although we spotted some groups of White Russians, they turned out to be harmless summer vacationists. The secretary of the Royan cell of the Communist party, Gourbil, had a small bicycle store in Saint-Palais. As soon as we learned in mid-August that he opposed the Stalinist leadership of the party and that we could trust him, he was brought to the villa, where he became a regular visitor. Trotsky always enjoyed talking with him.

Gourbil told me that Marcel Cureaudau, a taxi driver in Royan and a member of the Communist party, had some measure of sympathy for the opposition, but that he himself did not know how far this sympathy went. If the man were brought to meet Trotsky, therefore, we ran the risk that he would talk and divulge the villa's secret. So we waited until the very last days of Trotsky's stay in Saint-Palais. One day in early October I went to Cureaudau's taxi and asked him if he wanted to meet Trotsky. He was stunned. The visit went well; Trotsky was always eager to make contact with French workers. At the end of the conversation, Cureaudau asked Trotsky the inevitable question: "Comrade Trotsky, how did you lose power?" "Oh! You know, Comrade Cureaudau, one does not lose power in the same way that one loses a wallet." Then he launched into a description of what had happened in Russia at the time of Lenin's death. (Yet, if I may make a parenthetical comment, perhaps, in a sense, you do lose power as you lose your wallet. You are sure of having it; then suddenly you feel your pocket, you lose a vote or an election, it is no longer there and you cannot put your hand on it again. Moreover, there is always a question as to the sense in which Trotsky ever "had" power.)

Natalia came back from Paris on October 8 with Henri and Raymond Molinier. A vacation trip had been decided upon, since Trotsky needed a rest. On October 9 at eleven in the morning, Trotsky and Natalia left Saint-Palais by car with Henri Molinier and Jean Meichler. Trotsky had shaved his goatee, to make himself less conspicuous. Traveling through Bordeaux and Mont-de-Marsan, the travelers reached Bagnères-de-Bigorre in the High Pyrenees, where they settled down in a hotel. The other occupants of the Sea Spray villa left for Paris. That was the end of the Saint-Palais episode.

With Bagnères-de-Bigorre as their base, Trotsky and Natalia went on short trips in various directions. Thus they happened to visit Lourdes, and Trotsky himself later gave his impressions of this visit in his diary entry of April 29, 1935: "A shop for miracles, a business office for trafficking in grace . . . Indeed, the thinking of mankind is bogged down in its own excrement." Henri Molinier had left the group and gone back to Paris, to prepare a new residence for Trotsky. Jeanne Martin, I believe, spent a few days with the vacationists. During these three weeks of rest Trotsky did not write a single line, as far as I know; he only read the newspapers.

On October 31, 1933, at five o'clock in the afternoon the travelers took the bus from Bagnères-de-Bigorre to Tarbes, and from there, at

The Ker Monique villa in Barbizon.

eleven o'clock at night, the train for Orléans. The next morning Raymond Molinier was waiting for them in Orléans with a car. Meichler went back to Paris, while Raymond took Trotsky and Natalia to Barbizon. On the same day, November 1, I too arrived in Barbizon from Paris with Henri Molinier.

Barbizon was much closer than Saint-Palais to Paris. Although no explicit restrictions were attached to the visa that the French government had granted Trotsky, his place of residence had to be approved by the authorities. I do not think that they would have allowed him to live in Paris, fearing that he would take too great a part in daily political activities. But the stay in Saint-Palais had gone so well that Henri Molinier had ventured to present the French authorities with a proposal that he reside in Barbizon, thirty miles southeast of Paris, which had been accepted. Barbizon seemed a reasonable compromise: it was not Paris, but neither was it far away.

Barbizon was then a very small town in the department of Seine-et-Marne on the edge of the Fontainebleau forest. Although painters had made the town known, it was still an extremely quiet place. Henri Molinier had rented a villa on a country road that ran beside the forest. The house, called the Ker Monique, had two stories, and Trotsky's bedroom and study were located on the second floor. The rooms were small, the stairs and corridors narrow. We felt extremely cramped, having nothing like the space we had enjoyed in Prinkipo or Saint-Palais. The garden too was not large. The villa was hardly more than a suburban cottage, but the place was out of the way and very quiet. When I went back to Barbizon in 1973, the road beside the forest had not changed, but the villa had been torn down to make way for a more spacious house.

After a few days we had settled in. Besides Trotsky and Natalia, the permanent occupants of the house were Rudolf Klement, Sara Jacobs, Gabrielle Brausch, who had become my companion, and myself. Liova, Jeanne, and Henri came frequently by car. The wife of the Italian Trotskyite Blasco — we called her la Blascotte — came once a week to help Gaby and Natalia keep the house in order. Nobody else entered the house. Even in Paris, the French Trotskyites, with few exceptions, did not know where Trotsky was living.

The local authorities in Barbizon, the mayor in particular, had not been informed that Trotsky was living in the town. There was no direct police surveillance of the Ker Monique villa for quite some time. For our part, we could not keep watch at night, because there were only two men, Rudolf Klement and I, and with our other tasks, night duty was physically impossible. We put our trust in our incognito, the dogs, and the arrangement of rooms inside the house. I slept in a room near the door.

In the spring of 1933 Trotsky had vacillated between several projects for a new book, and in Saint-Palais, he had continued to think about writing a book on the Red Army. At the end of August, he described the subject of that book in a letter to an American literary agent. But a few days later, a British literary agent suggested to him that he write a book on Lenin, and after some hesitation, that idea prevailed.

Once settled in Barbizon, Trotsky started work on the project. Liova brought him books from Paris, especially Russian ones. I believe that Boris Nikolaievsky helped Liova to find these books. While reading them, Trotsky would mark certain passages with a very fine pencil line in the margin. These passages were then typed in Paris. Back in Barbizon, these excerpts, together with clippings and miscellaneous documents, were classified in folders. During the winter the work progressed regularly and several chapters were written.

At first Trotsky and Natalia took afternoon walks in the Fontainebleau forest, just in front of the villa. But with the coming of winter, the forest was no longer very pleasant; so on winter afternoons Trotsky and I went for short walks in the streets of Barbizon. The inhabitants of the small town, who from behind their windows would watch us pass by, had no inkling that this middle-aged man, with a still lively gait, was Trotsky. "To dress up, to eat — all these miserable petty things that one has to repeat from day to day!" he complained to me one day when we were walking on Barbizon's main street. On another day he told me: "Politics is the science of perspectives. This is what the French mean by calling it the science of measure. But for them, the measure is a small measure."

On one of these occasions he also spoke to me about his autobiography. Because Rieder, the French publisher, was planning to issue an abbreviated version, about one-third of the original text, Trotsky had reread his work and marked with pencil in the margin those passages that were to constitute the short edition. Without this reason for doing so, he would never have reread his own work. In a conversation with me on one of our walks, he criticized the book: "It's badly written. There are many things that should have been said and are not there. On the other hand, there are things there that should not have been included."

Trotsky was always complaining about misprints. The Trotskyite publications, often printed under difficult circumstances, were generally full of printer's errors. In his correspondence Trotsky frequently railed at those who were responsible, and in conversations he often returned to the subject. But he, himself, never read the proofs of his writings in Russian, whether books or articles. Liova took charge of that chore. Thus it came about that some instructions for the Russian typist, written by Trotsky lightly in pencil on the final manuscript of the *History of the Russian Revolution,* found themselves incorporated into the printed text. Trotsky spoke to me about this mishap during one of our walks through Barbizon and seemed quite irritated by what had happened. Of all his books, however, he undoubtedly ranked the *History* highest, and except for these printing errors he had no criticisms of it.

Benno and Stella were installed in two doghouses in the garden of the villa, and Trotsky took it upon himself to care for them. He always brought them their food. One night, Benno started to howl incessantly for no apparent reason, as dogs sometimes do. I went out to quiet him, but to no avail. Some neighbors called us on the telephone, complaining about the noise and threatening to summon the police. The situation was fast becoming awkward. Suddenly, in the middle of the night, Trotsky came down from his room, took a leash, and went out to Benno, shouting and lashing. The dog took refuge in his kennel. For quite some time Trotsky continued to strike at the doghouse with the leash, while shouting insults at Benno in Russian. The howling stopped.

Soon there were trips to Paris. We usually went every second or third Sunday, but at times every Sunday. At the beginning, Liova and Henri Molinier would come by car on those Sunday mornings and drive away with Trotsky. But soon things were done more simply. Trotsky and I walked together to the Fontainebleau highway, where we hailed the bus for Paris. While on the bus, Trotsky kept a handkerchief over the lower part of his face, as if he had a cold, to hide his goatee, which he had let grow again after his return from the Pyrenees. After a time Rudolf Klement and I decided to take turns accompanying him. In Paris some friends had put five or six apartments at Liova's disposal, which we used in rotation. Chief among the persons whom Trotsky met under these conditions were Trotskyite leaders, French or foreign, who either lived in Paris or had come there specially to see him. For a time Trotsky even took part more or less regularly in meetings of the International Secretariat. He met German and Austrian political refugees, in particular Willi Schlamm. He renewed relations, personal and political, with Ruth Fischer and Maslow. He also met Simone Weil, with whom he had a heated discussion on the nature of the Soviet state.

In the evening after the talks had ended, Trotsky sometimes took a walk through the streets of Paris before returning to Barbizon. He would walk down the Boulevard Saint-Michel, with Liova on his right and me on his left. Keeping his handkerchief over his goatee, he would stop to look at the bookstore windows.

On November 7, 1933, Liova and Jeanne came for dinner in Barbizon. There was a bottle of French wine on the table. As Trotsky and Natalia sat in the small dining room of that suburban cottage amid its hideous furniture, reunited with their son and less isolated than in Turkey, they were unwittingly living the least difficult hours of their entire exile.

At the end of January 1934, Sara Jacobs suddenly decided to go back to New York to be with her husband. She left before a replacement could be arranged. On February 20, three weeks after she stopped working, Trotsky was still writing to Liova, in German: "Meine Arbeit ist sehr desorganisiert [My work is very disorganized]."

On February 6, 1934, riots were provoked on the Place de la Concorde by right-wing groups against the Daladier government, after which the left counterattacked with a huge demonstration on February 12. France was entering a process of political polarization. In Paris, the Trotskyite group was trying to move beyond purely propagandistic activities, and new possibilities of action were opening up. All forces were needed. It was decided that I should go to work in the organization in Paris, returning to Barbizon once or twice a week to handle the French correspondence. Gaby came with me to Paris, and her place in Barbizon was taken by Trude, the wife of Otto Schüssler, who was himself living in Paris. Rudolf Klement stayed on in Barbizon. Max Gawenski, a Polish Trotskyite whose knowledge of Russian was far from perfect, went at times to Barbizon to type in Russian. The whole situation was not very satisfactory for Trotsky's work. But it did not last long.

Trotsky had a side to him that was didactic, at times pedantic, one could almost say conservative. He looked askance at any innovation in the field of Marxist theory. He had an expression for such innovations: "to trim Marx's beard." In February 1933 in Prinkipo he had asked Pierre Frank and me to put together all the theses and resolutions adopted by the first four congresses of the Communist International. His plan was to use them exactly as they were, so that they would constitute a kind of chart for the international Trotskyite organization. Once the texts had been collected, it became obvious that, besides dealing with broad political perspectives, they covered so many narrow, out-of-date problems that it would be impossible to use them unchanged for a new program. The project had to be abandoned. On March 13, 1934, Trotsky finished an article on military questions and the war of the future, in which he wrote, "However, in spite of the motorization of transportation and military devices, the need of an army for horses remains unchanged: as in Napoleon's time, one horse is needed for three soldiers." At the very moment when Trotsky was writing these lines, a French major was about to herald the role that tanks would play in the coming war.

Although the Sûreté Générale had not informed the local authorities of Trotsky's presence in Barbizon, the household in the Ker Monique villa was so different from an ordinary French family that by January 1934 it had attracted the attention of the French gendarmes, alerted by gossip in Barbizon. I learned later that some residents of Barbizon had even suspected the villa of sheltering a gang of counterfeiters. Why? Because we were buying more milk than the average French family, and clandestine printers apparently drink a lot of milk to overcome the toxic effects of lead. Hence, in the small town of Barbizon, scandalmongers were busy. The gendarmes had observed nothing with which they could incriminate the occupants of the villa, but they still wondered who these people were and what they were doing.

On April 12, 1934, at eleven in the evening, Rudolf Klement was returning to Barbizon on a motorbike, having spent the day in Paris, visited Liova, and picked up the mail, which he was bringing back. Two gendarmes stopped him on the pretext that his headlight was out of order. They asked him for the registration card of the motorbike. This card was not in his name but, I think, in mine. They charged him with using a stolen motorbike. Klement was carrying letters from all over the world and many foreign newspapers. He could not clearly explain who he was or where he was going, and he spoke French with a heavy German accent. All this was more than enough to make him suspect, and the gendarmes arrested him.

On April 13, the Melun district attorney and the prefect of Seine-et-Marne put their heads together to decide what to do. It was obvious, from the letters seized, that Trotsky was involved. So, before taking any action, the Melun district attorney telephoned the Ministry of the Interior to inquire about the conditions of Trotsky's sojourn in France. He was told that Trotsky was in France on a perfectly regular visa, but that he was supposed to be in Corsica. What lay behind this mistake? It is difficult to say. After the February disturbances, the Daladier government had given way to a government headed by the senile Doumergue, which was much further to the right. With the change of administration, many top officials had been replaced, especially in the Ministry of the Interior. It is possible that a new official, unfamiliar with the Trotsky dossier, taken by surprise over the telephone and remembering vaguely what the newspapers had published upon Trotsky's arrival in

France, could have answered that Trotsky should be in Corsica. At the Sûreté, Henri Molinier was restricted to dealing with very few officials, and Trotsky's place of residence was confidential information, not to be found in many folders. One or two persons knew about it, but the official who answered the telephone was doubtless not au courant.

On April 14 in the morning, the Melun district attorney arrived at the Ker Monique villa, accompanied by gendarmes, Klement in handcuffs, and a clerk, in order to interrogate Trotsky about the affair of the motorbike. The charge of theft could not, of course, be maintained. Trotsky himself wrote about this visit in his diary entries of March 18 and 21, 1935. Whatever may have been the exact reasons behind the official's report that Trotsky should have been in Corsica, the French Government seized the opportunity. It took advantage of this local incident, which it had perhaps not wanted but was now quite happy to exploit, in order to modify the conditions of Trotsky's residence in France. The Daladier government, after granting Trotsky a visa, had seemed hardly to bother about what he was doing. But now with the Doumergue government, this situation had become something of an anachronism. Everybody began shouting that Trotsky should have been in Corsica. The press launched a hysterical campaign. The newspapers demanded that Trotsky "go back" to Corsica, where he had never been, or that more stringent measures be taken against him.

Long before the Barbizon affair, Liova had rented in Lagny, a small town in the department of Seine-et-Marne about eighteen miles east of Paris, a villa where he rarely went but which he kept in reserve. Only two or three persons around him knew about the existence of the villa. On the evening of April 15, Henri Molinier and Liova hurriedly drove Trotsky and Natalia from Barbizon to Lagny. I remained in the Ker Monique villa all alone. Reporters arrived. Soon at least a dozen of them were keeping watch around the house during the day, and at night they occupied Barbizon's small hotel. Curiosity seekers also started to come, and the little town experienced an unusual bustle. I made believe that Trotsky and Natalia were still living in the villa. I would open up the shutters of their rooms on the second floor in the morning and close them at night. To my astonishment, the comedy succeeded. The reporters never saw anybody but me, which should have seemed strange to them; but as Trotsky was not reported to be anywhere else, nothing

Jean van Heijenoort chatting with reporters in Barbizon, April 1934.

"Curiosity seekers also started to come . . . ," Barbizon, April 1934.

shook their certitude that he still was in the Ker Monique villa. Shortly I began to read in the morning newspapers details that I had given by telephone on the day before to Liova or Raymond Molinier, and I realized that the reporters had connected a field telephone to our line at some distance from the villa. It then became quite easy to deceive them. I would simply give fictitious details in a confidential manner over the telephone. As I had taken the name of Marcel, the newspapers were soon full of Marcel's doings.

During the week, hardly anyone other than the journalists loitered around the villa; but on Sunday, there was always a crowd. As I remember, special bus trips from Paris to Barbizon were even organized. One Sunday afternoon, a crowd of several hundred persons was milling around the villa. The woods behind the house had been invaded. There were shouts and insults. It was a typical idle holiday crowd, ready for anything. I was alone in the house, with Benno and Stella. The two gendarmes stationed outside were helpless against so many people. A fellow started to climb the fence. I dashed out toward him with Benno. He shouted to me that he was in his own country, in France, and that he could do as he pleased. I answered him that I was also in mine. Surprised to hear me speak without an accent, as he had expected to find a foreigner, he stopped, disconcerted, on top of the fence. The sight of Benno, growling at my side, perhaps inspired him with some wisdom, for he climbed back down on the other side.

During all the years that I spent with Trotsky, this was perhaps the only time that I knew fear. The newspapers had mounted a campaign against Trotsky. Passions were high. Everyone still thought that Trotsky was in the villa, and I was staying there every night all alone. One morning, after perhaps a dozen days of siege, I approached the group of reporters and announced to them that Trotsky had long since left and was now far away. They were not unduly angry with me for having tricked them. It had been a good fight.

Meanwhile, after a few days in Lagny, Trotsky had left with Meichler for Chamonix, where he lived in a hotel, not knowing exactly what would happen from one day to the next. Natalia had remained in Paris. Henri Molinier was pursuing negotiations with the French authorities about a new place of residence. There was talk of sending Trotsky to Madagascar or to Réunion Island. The Turkish government, discreetly sounded out about the possibility of Trotsky's return to Turkey, let it be known that this would not be allowed. For Trotsky, it was truly the planet without a visa.

At the beginning of May 1934, Natalia, Raymond Molinier, and I left Paris one morning by car and met Trotsky and Meichler in Chamonix. There followed a few hectic days. Since we were not far from the Swiss border, the Sûreté thought that we were trying to get into Switzerland. They gave the plate number of our car to a reporter, who had it published. This was a kind of warning, to make us respect certain stipulations, one of which was not to get too close to a border. Finally on May 10, with the agreement of the Sûreté, Trotsky, Natalia, and I settled down in a guest house, the Gombault pension in La Tronche, a small town near Grenoble. I registered under my own name. Trotsky and Natalia registered as my uncle and aunt. My name was foreign enough to explain the accent and manners of Trotsky and Natalia. In order to avoid meals at the table d'hôte, Trotsky and Natalia feigned a recent bereavement. Natalia dressed in black, and a black armband had been sewed on the sleeve of Trotsky's jacket. They both had their meals in their room, and when they went out, people whom they passed on their way through the house observed a respectful silence. Because the boardinghouse was small and had a much more familial atmosphere than a hotel, it would have been quite hard, without this trick, not to have been drawn into conversation, which might have awakened suspicion.

I took my meals at the table d'hôte, trying to observe insofar as possible what was going on around me. An "insurance agent" had come to the pension at about the same time we had. He was in fact a detective from the Sûreté, whose name was Gagneux. We had been informed of his presence, since the Sûreté was at the moment as concerned as we were to preserve Trotsky's incognito. Gagneux and I pretended to strike up an acquaintance. Thus we could meet and talk without arousing suspicion. Most of the boarders were young men from Latin America who were studying at the University of Grenoble. The danger lay elsewhere.

The weather was beautiful. At times, Trotsky and Natalia sat out of the way in the garden. Trotsky read the newspapers and dictated a bit to me in French. In the afternoon we often took walks through the countryside, which was then relatively rural and quite pleasant. On one of these walks we suddenly found ourselves inside a graveyard. It was a cemetery for Russian émigrés. The gravestones bore, in Russian, the names of colonels and generals. Trotsky walked by quickly, saying nothing.

We soon learned that the landlady was a practicing Catholic as well as a royalist. Gagneux, in doing his detective work, had gathered this information, which he imparted to me. Thus there arose the question of Sunday mass. When Sunday came around, Gagneux, who was a Freemason, nevertheless went out as if he were on his way to mass — all this in order to protect the incognito of Leon Trotsky in a royalist boardinghouse. Truly a Feydeau comedy! We ourselves deemed it advisable to take a walk on Sunday mornings at the time of mass. One Sunday morning, we even entered a church for ten minutes, probably the Saint-André church near Grenette Square, well known to Stendhal. The sermon was in progress. Trotsky listened for a few minutes. After we had left, he asked me, "Does he speak as well as Gérard?" Gérard Rosenthal was, among all the Paris Trotskyites, the one most noted for his oratorical skill.

In the living room of the guest house, which was available to all boarders, there were newspapers and magazines. One morning I found the latest issue of *L'Illustration,* with a beautiful picture of Trotsky and Natalia. The Barbizon affair had precipitated the publication of this picture. In the print, Trotsky had a goatee and his hair was combed back, whereas at the pension he was now shaved and his hair was parted on the side. Natalia, however, looked about the same as she did in the portrait. Even if there could have been doubts about one or the other, no one who had seen the picture could fail to recognize the two of them. I alerted Gagneux. He took the magazine to his room. The landlady, I believe, asked him to return it, but he succeeded in keeping it till our departure. Trotsky himself gave a lively description of our stay in the guest house in his diary entry of May 8, 1935.

We left La Tronche on May 28. Raymond Molinier had rented a house in Saint-Pierre-de-Chartreuse, a godforsaken village in the Alps, some twenty miles north of Grenoble. I left for Paris to take my place in the French Trotskyite group. Trotsky and Natalia settled down in Saint-Pierre with Raymond Molinier and Vera Lanis. The only other person staying with them in the house for a time was Max Gawenski, to type in Russian. It was supposed to be a stay of indefinite length.

I went from Paris to Saint-Pierre in the middle of June to bring the mail. My impression of the situation was not good. The village was very small, and a household of newcomers could not fail to attract attention. Moreover, Raymond Molinier's qualities were not such as could allow him to adapt himself to daily life with Trotsky in a small house. Gawenski, besides being poor as a Russian typist, did not get along well with people. Anyway, the arrangement did not last.

While Trotsky was in Saint-Pierre, I made a trip to Holland and one to Belgium. The people around Trotsky always had two plans of travel in reserve, called in code Operation Parijanine and Operation Marguerite. The first plan was for Trotsky to move from one country to another in a perfectly legal manner. The second plan was to do the same operation illegally. In June 1934, because of the difficulties of Trotsky's residence in France, Liova and I undertook to reactivate Operation Marguerite. I therefore went to Holland to meet Sneevliet and find in his party a Dutchman of the same height, age, and general appearance as Trotsky. We then brought the Dutchman openly to France and took him back out of France surreptitiously, so that the French police could not stamp his passport as having left the country. The whole operation was executed without mishap, and so we had, in Paris, a passport in reserve. Then I went to Brussels to see Henri Spaak, the leader of an opposition group inside the Socialist party who had shown some sympathy for Trotskyism, although his sympathy would not last long. Georges Vereeken, a Belgian Trotskyite, was with me, and Spaak received us in his study. He had harsh words for the leaders of the Socialist party: "They can go straight to the devil for all I care!" I explained to him the problem of getting Trotsky across the French-Belgian border in case of need. "No problem at all," he retorted. "I would go with my car to fetch him and, at the border, I would show my credentials as an elected representative."

In the summer of 1934, Trotsky made the suggestion that the French Trotskyite group enter the Socialist party. After Hitler's rise to power, the Stalinist calumnies against the Trotskyites had become more and more violent. The rank-and-file members of the French Communist party and Young Communist League were now so poisoned against us that it was impossible to have any kind of discussion with them; they immediately resorted to blows. Trotsky thought that if the Trotskyites entered the Socialist party they would be in a milieu in which they could function. The proposal, which became known as the French turn, provoked vigorous discussion in the French Trotskyite group as well as in the Trotskyite movement throughout the world. The days were not long past when the Trotskyites had considered themselves part of the Communist International. To enter the Socialist party was, for many of them, a psychological shock. Raymond Molinier and Naville split on the issue, Molinier being in favor of the entry and Naville against it. By the fall, the bulk of the French Trotskyite group was inside the Socialist party.

Trotsky had settled down in Saint-Pierre with the agreement of the Sûreté. In fact, the French authorities had given Trotsky and Natalia fictitious identification papers. Their name now appeared as Lanis, their nationality as Rumanian, and Trotsky's occupation as professor. "Lanis" was the actual name of Vera, Raymond Molinier's companion.

The Isère prefect, however, had his own reasons for not enjoying Trotsky's presence in his department, especially in Saint-Pierre, a village whose mayor, a devout Catholic, was a personal enemy of the prefect. If Trotsky's presence had been revealed, there would have been a scandal that would have reflected badly on the prefect. So he arranged a leak. The local newspapers published information that, without giving Trotsky's exact location, definitely pointed to the region. This was a form of blackmail: if Trotsky did not give up and leave, the information would become more specific.

At the end of June it therefore became necessary for him to leave Saint-Pierre. Trotsky, Natalia, and Raymond Molinier went to Grenoble, and I hurried there from Paris. We had no plans for a new place to stay, and were at an impasse. We had to start from scratch again. Raymond left for Paris to work out a solution. To make the problem of maintaining the incognito easier, Natalia went with him, while Trotsky and I took the bus to Lyons, where we signed into a hotel.

While there, we ate in restaurants. During the day, Trotsky read the newspapers, and we walked a great deal through the city. Trotsky developed the habit of going to a movie in the evening. We also bought a few books. One afternoon when we were in a public library, Trotsky asked for a book by Fourier, and we stayed there reading for two or three hours. Later, when I was in New York during World War II, I told this story to André Breton, who was very interested, and it perhaps incited him to write his *Ode à Fourier*. On another day while Trotsky and I were walking in the streets of Lyons, an unemployed worker begged us for money. "Give him something," Trotsky told me. I gave the worker a two-franc coin. "Give him more," Trotsky urged me. So I gave the worker a five-franc bill. Trotsky never had any money on him. He lived in countries without ever knowing the color of their bills.

Often we sat in parks. One day while we were resting in a park and watching children at play, a mother gave her child a slap in the face. "That's the dialectic of love and hatred," Trotsky observed. Later in Mexico City, as we were coming out of the dentist's one day, Trotsky told me, "There ought to be a synthetic mode of treating a tooth." These were his ways of finding Marxist dialectics in daily life. While resting on park benches, Trotsky occasionally dictated letters or notes to me. Raymond visited us once, bringing the mail, which had to be answered, and work continued somehow. But in general during these days Trotsky was taciturn and ill at ease. The instability of his situation was beginning to weigh on him.

While Trotsky and I were in Lyons, Henri and Raymond Molinier strove to find a solution to the problem of our living arrangements — Henri conducting negotiations with the French authorities, Raymond looking for a suitable place. Soon a solution emerged. After the Barbizon affair, I had gone to see Maurice Dommanget, one of the leaders of the schoolteachers' union, in the small village of the Oise department where he was teaching. Like quite a few of his colleagues in the union, Dommanget had sympathy for Trotsky, even though he was not a Trotskyite. I had asked him if he could find a schoolteacher, living in a fairly large house in a village or small town far from Paris, who would be willing to shelter Trotsky in exchange for rent. Dommanget told me that he would look. Thus it came about that at the beginning of July he proposed the house of Laurent Beau in Domène, a small town some six miles east of Grenoble. Raymond Molinier went to Domène to survey the situation. Everything was satisfactory. Laurent Beau's three-story house, surrounded by a large garden, was on the Route de Savoie, somewhat off the road, about one mile from the center of Domène. Beau, although not a Trotskyite, was a left-wing schoolteacher, and he stood ready to rent part of his house to Trotsky.

Trotsky, Natalia, and I arrived in Domène shortly before mid-July 1934. Henri Molinier brought us there by car. The initial arrangements in the house were makeshift. Trotsky worked, I believe, in Beau's study on the ground floor. Because it was out of the question to have a Russian typist, Trotsky took to writing in longhand. After a period during which we took our meals with the Beaus, Natalia began to prepare small meals for Trotsky and herself alone, with some help from Marguerite Beau. I ate out most of the time. As I had a bicycle, it was easy to ride to the center of Domène. Gagneux, the Sûreté agent, had also settled in Domène and kept an eye on the house. His watch was for two purposes. On the one hand, he had to make sure that Trotsky's incognito was not disturbed; on the other hand, he had to keep track of Trotsky's visitors.

The house had no immediate neighbors. In the back, the garden rose directly into the foothills of the Alps. Trotsky and Natalia could go for walks unaccompanied in that direction, certain not to meet anybody. In the evening Beau occasionally took us out for a ride in his small car. We would drive through the countryside for an hour or less, without stopping. Trotsky and Natalia sat in the back, while I stayed up front next to Beau. The conversation with Beau was always meager.

In Grenoble there was a young teacher, Alexis Bardin, who had strong Trotskyite sympathies; he even had two brothers in the Trotskyite group in Paris, one of whom, Boitel, played a leading role there. Alexis Bardin and his wife, Violette, were soon authorized by the Isère prefect to visit Trotsky and Natalia. Bardin, who was a member of the Socialist party, was involved in Grenoble's political and trade union life. The conversations between Trotsky and him revolved around local politics. Trotsky was interested in the smallest details, enjoying the chance to immerse himself in practical day-to-day activities. Bardin was becoming more and more active in local affairs, and some of his speeches at trade union meetings were written by Trotsky. A few years earlier, before Hitler's rise to power in Germany, Trotsky had similarly written the speeches of a German Trotskyite, Seipold, which were delivered in the Prussian Landtag.

The political situation in France was growing more and more tense as the country became increasingly polarized between left and right, and there was a great deal to be done in the Trotskyite group in Paris. It was therefore decided that I should share my time between Domène and Paris. I would spend three or four weeks in Paris, then the same amount of time in Domène. This schedule was not fixed but varied with the needs of the day. During October 1934 I was in Domène, translating the first part of *Whither France?* into French. As Trotsky wrote, I translated. The pamphlet, which analyzed the political situation in France, could not be published under Trotsky's name without further compromising his position with the French authorities. My translation was therefore arranged so as to obliterate the most salient marks of his style, and the text was published in *La Vérité* as having been written jointly by a number of French Trotskyites. The Russian manuscript nevertheless had to be preserved, so Natalia sewed it into the lining of my jacket as I was to leave for Paris.

I was in Domène during January 1935, helping Trotsky with another pamphlet. On December 1, 1934, Kirov, the secretary of the Communist party in Leningrad, had been shot in rather mysterious circumstances by a young terrorist, Nikolaiev, whose motive remained unknown. Stalin unleashed a new campaign of calumnies against the Trotskyites and had several dozen G.P.U functionaries shot. Trotsky was trying to unravel, with the information then at his disposal, the mechanism of what he considered a plot of Stalin's. I translated into French as he wrote, and shortly afterward, the pamphlet was published in Paris. In a conversation with me at the time, Trotsky sketched his theory of what he called "crowned socialism." "You will see, Stalin will get himself crowned." He thought that, after the Kirov assassination, Stalin would assume some majestic title, like Bonaparte adopting the name of Napoleon. In a way, this is what happened when Stalin later designated himself the "Father of the Peoples" and surrounded himself with a halo of Byzantine adulation, launching the cult of personality. Kirov's assassination and its consequences thus marked an important stage in the construction of the myth. But Trotsky may have been thinking of a return to something more traditional and formal.

At the end of January while I was still in Domène, my son was born near Paris. Raymond Molinier gave me the news during one of the telephone conversations that I had almost every evening with him from Grenoble. Raymond thought it would be a good joke to tell me that Gaby had delivered twins. Since I had no reason to disbelieve him, I gave the news to Trotsky. "The mixture of races is always very fertile," he said immediately. Gaby was short and dark, I tall and blond. This difference was all that Trotsky needed to construct a theoretical explanation.

I was in Domène again in February, when Trotsky was writing the second part of *Whither France?* On February 7, he began his diary. This diary, which is a precious document for the study of Trotsky's personality, was written during a particularly difficult period in his exile, so that it would be deceptive to extrapolate the atmosphere and mood of the diary to the whole of the exile without reservation and modification. Moreover, Trotsky's relative involvement in his different interests as revealed in the diary is not what it was in reality. Trotsky knew that, if another incident occurred, his diary might well fall into the hands of the French authorities. So the text is full of little tricks. In the entry of April 9, for example, Trotsky writes that he "does not know" who wrote *Whither France?* It may even be that Trotsky, who a few months earlier during the Barbizon affair had called himself an "old conspirator," wrote the diary to some extent to have something to show to the French police: "Look, here is what I busy myself with!" A whole section of Trotsky's political activity therefore does not appear in the diary. His constant interventions in the factional fights of various Trotskyite groups all over the world, his political correspondence, and his visitors leave no trace at all in the diary. Liova, Jeanne, and Raymond Molinier frequently came from Paris. Besides them, other visitors came for political discussions. Thus Henryk Sneevliet, Pierre Naville, Jean Rous, and Marceau Pivert visited Domène. Yvan Craipeau also came one day, and to escape Gagneux's surveillance, Raymond Molinier had to hide him in the trunk of the car while driving him through the center of the town.

Two or three months after Trotsky's arrival in Domène, when it became clear that he was going to stay there some time, an effort was made to improve the living arrangements. Beau put a whole floor at the disposal of Trotsky and Natalia. One room was the bedroom, another was Trotsky's study. Shelves were installed in a corridor and books were sent from Paris. When I was in Domène, I worked and slept in a small room on the same floor. It had become necessary to install a bathroom on that floor, which entailed substantial expense. Neither Beau nor Trotsky had much money. In fact, Trotsky's financial situation was then rather difficult, for in the midst of his tribulations he was unable to write paid articles. Consequently there was some haggling over the share that each one should pay for the work. For a time, relations were strained; Trotsky and Beau no longer talked to each other. Later, shortly before Trotsky's departure, the situation improved. This episode provoked Trotsky to write in his diary on February 12, 1935: "There is no creature more disgusting than a petit bourgeois engaged in primitive accumulation. I have never had the opportunity to observe this type as closely as I do now." The remark reeks of anger. To speak of "primitive accumulation" in this connection is to misuse a category of Marxist economics. Beau was certainly not being transformed into a capitalist by the rent that Trotsky paid him. Natalia sounds a different note in her memoirs when she speaks of the Beaus as "these excellent people."

In May I took the train from Paris to Grenoble on my way to Domène.

The trip was long and the afternoon hot; so I went to the dining car to drink some mineral water. The waiter gave me a bill, which I slipped into the book I was reading, one of those I was bringing to Trotsky. The day after my arrival, as I was strolling in the garden near the house, Trotsky suddenly appeared at the window of his study and, waving the bill, shouted to me in French, "Oh, oh, you went on a binge in the dining car!" He knew a number of slang expressions in French, which he delighted in using. It was a good thing that I had drunk nothing stronger than mineral water!

Norway now had a Socialist government. Walter Held, a German Trotskyite who had taken refuge in Norway, organized some Norwegian friends to ask the government for a visa for Trotsky. On June 8, 1935, I arrived in Domène from Paris with the news that the Norwegian government had granted Trotsky permission to live in Norway. Although the visas had not yet been physically stamped into Trotsky's and Natalia's passports, because those passports were in Domène, it seemed that this would be a mere formality. In two days, Natalia and I had packed the clothes, manuscripts, and a few books, and we bade a brief farewell to the Beaus.

On the evening of June 10, we were at the Grenoble railroad station, ready to take the train for Paris. The head of the Sûreté in Grenoble was to accompany us. As we were about to step into the railroad car, he pointed out to me the Isère prefect, who, on another platform, was observing from a distance Trotsky's departure from his department. Trotsky and Natalia had a compartment to themselves and slept stretched out on the seats. I stood all night in the corridor by their door, and we arrived in Paris at dawn. Liova met us at the station. Trotsky and Natalia went immediately to the apartment of Gérard Rosenthal, where he lived with his father, a well-known Parisian doctor.

It then came to light that the Norwegian government was still hesitating, and for several days the negotiations were hectic. The French authorities wanted to see Trotsky out of the country as fast as possible and were clearly not disposed to allow a return to Domène. While the visa negotiations were under way, quite a few members of the Paris Trotskyite group also came to the apartment to discuss questions of political tactics with Trotsky, because the national congress of the

French Socialist party was then in session in Mulhouse, and the conflict of the French Trotskyites with the leadership of that party was coming to a head. Trotsky himself described these few hectic days in Paris in his diary entry of June 20, 1935, written shortly after the events. On June 13 matters were finally settled. The Norwegian visa was granted for six months, and we made ready to leave.

3. NORWAY

At a quarter past midnight on the night of June 13, 1935, Trotsky, Natalia, Jean Rous, and I took the train in the Gare du Nord for Antwerp. Rous, who was then one of the leaders of the French Trotskyites, came with us as far as Antwerp so that I would not have to do all of the guard duty alone; moreover, Trotsky wanted to talk with him about the problems of the French Trotskyite group. In the morning we arrived at Antwerp, where we were met by Jan Frankel, who had come from Czechoslovakia. We checked into the Hotel Excelsior. Whereas in this same city, in November 1932 the Belgian police had cordoned off the ship that was bringing Trotsky back from Denmark, in 1935 the police left us alone. The French police, too, had been extremely discrete in the Gare du Nord. The whole trip was a much simpler affair than Trotsky's previous journeys.

During June 14 and 15, Trotsky had conversations in Antwerp with several Belgian Trotskyites and also with members of a Flemish Socialist group called the Liga. At eight o'clock in the evening of June 15, Trotsky, Natalia, Frankel, and I sailed for Oslo on the Norwegian ship *Paris*. Rous had gone back to Paris. On the boat everything went smoothly and simply. The passengers, for the most part Norwegians, seemed to pay no attention to us. On June 18 in the morning the ship glided into Oslo Fjord. The immigration proceedings took little time. The disembarkation was routine: we simply walked down the gangplank in a group with all the other passengers. If there were reporters, they did not show themselves. We immediately left by car for Jevnaker, a small town about thirty miles northwest of Oslo, where we settled down for a few days in a small, immaculate hotel.

To guide us in this new world, we had Walter Held, whose real name was Heinz Epe, a German refugee who had settled in Norway a year or two earlier and whose wife was Norwegian. Besides him, we had a few Norwegian friends, in particular Olav Scheflo, a journalist who had

Trotsky on the Norwegian ship Paris *between Antwerp and Oslo, June 1935.*

*Natalia, an unidentified passenger, Trotsky,
and Jean van Heijenoort disembarking in Oslo, June 18, 1935.*

been very helpful in the matter of Trotsky's visa, and Kjell Ottesen, a university student. On June 23 Trotsky and Natalia took up residence in the house of Konrad Knudsen and his wife. Knudsen was then a member of the Norwegian parliament. The arrangement had been made through Scheflo, who was a friend of the Knudsens. The house, which was situated in unwalled grounds near a small wood, was large and comfortable, though not luxurious. Not far away were a few other houses. The hamlet, called Wexhall, was part of the town of Hønefoss, which was located some forty miles north of Oslo as the crow flies.

As the Knudsens could not allot more than a part of their house to Trotsky, he was to live there with a reduced secretariat and without a special guard. Jan Frankel was to be the only secretary. On June 25, therefore, I left for France by train. The books and archives that had been left in Domène were sent to Hønefoss at the end of July. The Russian typewriter was also sent, for a Russian typist had been found, and Trotsky could resume regular work.

During the leftist street demonstration of February 12, 1934, in Paris, Frankel had been spotted as an alien by a plainclothes policeman. After being arrested, he was expelled from France. Back in Prague, Frankel arranged for the deportation notice, which the French police had stamped in his passport, to be removed by a professional forger. With this passport, which was genuine though altered, he then entered Norway with Trotsky. In October 1935, as an alien residing in Norway, he was required to present himself to the Norwegian police for a routine registration. The alteration of the passport could have been detected, which would have caused a small scandal for Trotsky; so it was deemed advisable that Frankel return to Czechoslovakia. Back in Prague, he did what he could to find a substitute for himself in Hønefoss, selecting a Czechoslovakian Trotskyite, Erwin Wolf, who on November 15 arrived in Hønefoss. Frankel had spent several years with Trotsky, but Wolf had no such experience. He had no great liking for secretarial duties, and in subsequent months Trotsky's correspondence and manuscripts were not kept in the best of order.

Back in Paris, I took my place in the French Trotskyite group. Since the fall of 1934 the members of the group had been active in both the Socialist party and the Socialist youth organization, but they had achieved more success with the youth than in the party itself. The Trotskyites had recruited supporters among the young, and Fred Zeller's young Socialist group, which had maintained its leadership of the Seine district, had moved closer to them. At the time of my return, a sharp struggle was beginning to take place in the youth organization between the Trotskyites and Zeller's friends, on one side, and the more conservative elements, on the other.

At the end of July the national convention of the Young Socialists took place in Lille. On July 30 I sent Trotsky the following telegram from Lille: "National youth congress expelling us and Zeller faction." Our expulsion had been hatched by the right wing of the party, with the help of Stalinist sympathizers. On August 8 a group representing the expelled, which included Fred Zeller, David Rousset, Yvan Craipeau, myself, and a few others, met in the Socialist party headquarters with a commission composed of leaders of the Socialist party, including Léon

Blum. The commission wanted to play a conciliatory role, hoping that we would stay in the Socialist organization even though subjected to harsh conditions. We sat around a long, narrow table, with Blum seated almost opposite me. In his honeyed voice, but not without charm and with forceful argument, he tried to persuade us to accept the traditional Socialist position. But matters had gone too far, and there could be no turning back.

The Zeller group joined the Trotskyites to form a new independent youth organization. At the end of October, Zeller went to see Trotsky in Norway, where he stayed about two weeks. Inevitably, he asked Trotsky how he had lost power, adding, "Why did you not use the formidable apparatus that was under your control in order to resist?" Trotsky, though calling the question "naïve," nevertheless wrote a long article on the subject, dated November 12 and entitled "Why Did Stalin Defeat the Opposition?" which is perhaps the most complete and coherent presentation of his views, with their strong points as well as their weak ones. In particular, he stated: "There is no doubt that in those days a military coup d'état against the faction of Zinoviev, Kamenev, and Stalin presented no difficulties and would even have cost no bloodshed, but the results of such a coup d'état would have been an accelerated march toward the bureaucratization and bonapartization against which the Left Opposition had taken up the fight."

In his enthusiasm as a neophyte, Zeller sent a postcard from Norway to a Stalinist friend in Paris, in which he exclaimed, "Death to Stalin! Long live Trotsky!" The friend had nothing better to do than hand the postcard over to the leadership of the Communist party. The incident caused a small scandal, since all the Stalinists interpreted the postcard as a call to individual terrorism.

Toward the end of 1935, Trotsky entered into negotiations, through Liova, with the International Institute for Social History, located in Amsterdam, to sell to the Institute his correspondence for the years 1917-1922. There were almost nine hundred documents. The letters were copies, either typewritten or photographic, the originals having been deposited in Moscow on order of the Politburo. A sales contract was signed with the Institute on December 28, 1935.

On January 26, 1936, Liova sent his father a handwritten note in Russian concerning the correspondence he had delivered to the Amsterdam

Institute. In it he wrote: "I have withdrawn three documents by Lenin (and two photographs of two of these three documents; there was no photograph of the third one). In one, a telegram, he says, 'Do use both corruption and the threat of general extermination'; in the second, 'We shall kill off all of them if they set the oil afire'; and in the third he demands that the Ijevsk workers be shot for sabotage. Meanwhile, I am keeping these documents.'" This is the only case of interfering with documents that I know about in Trotsky's entourage, and here it was a question of protecting Lenin's memory.

I do not know what ever became of the documents that were withdrawn. I was not able to find them in Jan M. Meijer's book, *The Trotsky Papers, 1917-1922*. The only item that I did locate there was (page 545) the text of a telegram sent by Lenin to Skliansky on June 8, 1919, saying with respect to the Ijevsk workers, "Do send a telegram (over my signature) to Melnichansky stating that it would be a disgrace to hesitate and to fail to punish absences by executions," which seems to fit the third document described by Liova.

When Trotsky had proposed the entry of the French Trotskyite group into the Socialist party, Naville had disagreed and had abandoned the organization to form a small group of his own. Once the entry had been made, however, Naville decided that his group too would join the Socialist party. Within that party the two groups found themselves working more and more in common, and when it became necessary to reconstitute an independent Trotskyite group after the expulsions from the Socialist party in the fall of 1935, Naville became a leader of that group, together with Raymond Molinier, Pierre Frank, Jean Rous, Bardin (Boitel), and a few others.

In September or October 1935, Molinier was beginning to show signs of impatience with his collaborators. The Trotskyite group was making too little headway for his taste, and the newspaper published by the group, *La Vérité*, was in his view too abstract to reach the workers. Lines began to form, and the organization split into two factions. I found myself on the side of Raymond Molinier. Since first entering the Trotskyite movement, I had been politically connected with him in the various internal embroilments of the French group. He had enjoyed Trotsky's confidence since 1929. Nobody had as much energy as he.

When events demanded quick action, Raymond Molinier was always there, willing to find money, to print a poster, to organize a meeting. Out of a kind of bravado that was customary with him, Raymond Molinier sent Trotsky a letter showing his hand. In it he described his projects in a detail that he had not yet given to those around him, at least not to me. During those same days I wrote to Trotsky describing the situation as I saw it. Since I did not mention in my letter the exact plans that Molinier had just sketched to him, for the good reason that I was unaware of them, Trotsky thought I was trying to deceive him. As if I were not in the best position to know that such would be impossible! He received information from all sides; for Liova and several others wrote to him regularly.

The break occurred at the beginning of December. The Molinier-Frank group, of which I was a member, began publishing a new newspaper, *La Commune*. Jeanne Martin also belonged to this group, which was to create complications between Liova and herself that, as the years went by, became more and more painful. In those weeks, however, the split had not yet gone much beyond the kind of factional fighting that had always taken place. Negotiations were carried on between the two groups. As for me, my relations with Trotsky were interrupted, which affected me deeply.

As it turned out, *La Commune* made no more headway than *La Vérité*. Both were confronting the same difficulties, and there was no magic formula for success. In the first half of January 1936, I abandoned what now seemed to me to be an aimless adventure. For a few weeks, I drifted, separate from both groups. Then I rejoined the official Trotskyite group in mid-February. Gaby, who, like me, had chosen the Molinier group at the time of the split, stayed in it, which created, between her and me, a situation somewhat similar to that existing between Jeanne and Liova.

My political tribulations had further repercussions on my personal life. Being separated from both groups, I had to look for a job. With the help of André Thirion, whom I had known in the Socialist party group of the nineteenth Paris district, I got a job doing actuarial work for France Mutualiste, a company that paid life annuities to veterans of World War I and had a staff of about two hundred. Thirion, though not at the top, held a fairly important position and had been able to hire a number of young Surrealists. At this time I also resumed my correspondence with Trotsky. As soon as the little book that André Gide had written after his trip to Russia, *Return from the U.S.S.R.*, came out, I sent it to Trotsky.

In the second half of May a wave of strikes broke all over France, in which the workers occupied the factories. On one particular evening at the beginning of June, a strange atmosphere hovered over Paris. The police were nowhere to be seen. The streets were empty, except for small groups of workers going from one occupied factory to another. But this situation did not last long. Negotiations began, and the city again took on a familiar face. On June 7, an accord was signed, which became known as the Matignon agreement, between the government, the employers, and the trade unions.

Then on Monday, June 8, France Mutualiste went on strike. We occupied the offices. During the day, women did the cooking. At night, we slept on the floor. Everything was done in good humor and with perfect discipline. I was secretary of the strike committee, which took possession of the director's office. Two police officers came to the gate, politely asking for figures on how many strikers there were, and one of them wrote the number in a notebook. This strike was, of course, only a drop of water in the wave of strikes that had swept over the country. In the microcosm of the strike at France Mutualiste, negotiations took the form of interminable meetings between the director and his aides, on one side, and the strike committee, on the other, around a huge desk. The strike was settled with significant salary raises, paid vacations, and other gains.

From Norway Trotsky was closely watching the situation in France. The French Trotskyite group had just gone through a process of reorganization. On June 1, a reconciliation, which was to last only a few months, was effected with the Molinier group; a new name was chosen, the Parti Ouvrier Internationaliste, or International Workers party; and a search was begun for a name for the party newspaper. On June 10 Trotsky wrote me: "Enclosed herewith is a new article, which I deem very URGENT. I am asking you to perform the impossible so that it will immediately be placed in the hands of our comrades and appear in the newspaper. The best name for the newspaper is *Le Soviet*. This will give

Trotsky and Natalia at the house in Wexhall, summer 1936.

us the opportunity to penetrate the ranks of the Communist workers, and, moreover, it fits the situation perfectly. As masthead: 'The soviets everywhere? Yes! But first in France.' "

The article in Russian that Trotsky enclosed with the letter was entitled "The French Revolution Has Begun," dated June 9; it was the continuation of another article written by him on the situation in France, entitled "The Decisive Step," dated June 5, which he had sent me a few days before. As for the exclamation "The soviets everywhere!" it was then the most popular slogan in the demonstrations organized by the Communist party. In not only proposing a title but thinking of a masthead, Trotsky showed his concern for details. I translated his article that night, seated at the desk of the director of France Mutualiste.

Trotsky's proposals were not accepted, however, and he began to show more and more impatience with the leadership of the French Trotskyite group. He thought that the group was not working with the urgency that the situation demanded, as he saw it. On June 12, he wrote me: "I received your note [telling of the strike at France Mutualiste] and I congratulate the secretary of the strike committee. I hope that you have given my *second* article [the one of June 9] to the editorial board. If this board does not accept the stipulation that I demand [to publish

Trotsky's articles without delay and without change], I shall publicly de-
clare that I assume no special responsibility for the organ of the French
section [of the international Trotskyite movement], and I shall maintain
contact with our comrades through *a weekly bulletin, of a few pages, in
which I can speak with full freedom*."

In view of the value that Trotsky ordinarily placed in the established
organization of the Trotskyite movement and the close attention with
which he had followed the formation of this particular group, it was
extraordinary for him to project a new bulletin. But he went even
further. Shortly afterward, I received a handwritten note from him, of
which no copy has been preserved and whose original has unfortunately
been lost, proposing the publication in Paris of a new newspaper,
called *Le Soviet*. Trotsky was to send me from Norway almost the entire
contents of each issue, and I was to translate the texts in Paris and take
care of the printing. A kind of neutrality was to be maintained with respect to the leadership of the French Trotskyite group. Trotsky had
apparently selected me for this project for the following reasons: I was
able to translate his articles quickly from Russian into French; I had
some experience with printing; and because of my short-lived membership in the Molinier group and then my break with them, I had no
strong political connections with either the Rous-Bardin-Naville team
or the Molinier-Frank team, the two groups then constituting the leadership of the French Trotskyites. The project of an independent newspaper, however, remained stillborn, as the wave of strikes subsided and
Trotsky's relations with the leadership of the French group took a turn
for the better.

On July 19, the Spanish Civil War broke out. Toward the end of the
month Trotsky let Liova know that he would like to go to Catalonia
clandestinely. Liova and I formed several plans. We thought of em-
ploying a fishing boat to take him from Norway to Spain, but nothing
came of the idea beyond a few conversations.

On August 5, Trotsky put the last touches to the manuscript of a book
on which he had been working for some time, *The Revolution Betrayed*,
and sent it to his translators. On the same day he left Wexhall with
Konrad Knudsen for an excursion near Christiansand. During that
night, members of the small pro-Nazi Norwegian group invaded the
Knudsen house and seized letters and documents belonging to Trotsky.

In Paris, Liova, who was worried about Trotsky's safety, asked me to leave for Norway. I took the boat in Antwerp and arrived in Oslo on the morning of August 25.

The ship was still floating on the calm waters of Oslo Fjord when the Norwegian morning newspapers were brought aboard. I could make out the headlines and thus learned the outcome of the first Moscow trial: Zinoviev, Kamenev, and fourteen other defendants had been shot. In Wexhall, where I settled in at once with Trotsky, Natalia, Erwin Wolf, and the Knudsen family, journalists called us up at all hours to obtain statements from Trotsky on the Moscow trial. Trotsky was worried, first by the trial itself, and then by its possible effects on the Norwegian government, which was taking a harsher and harsher attitude toward him. Moscow was exerting more and more pressure on the government, demanding that measures be taken against Trotsky and threatening, if these were not taken, to cut off its large imports of Norwegian herring.

On August 28, Trotsky went to Oslo with Erwin Wolf, in order to testify in the case of the Norwegian Nazis who had invaded the Knudsen house. The prosecution of these fascists took the form of an action against Trotsky. Called as a witness, he found himself turned into a defendant. During the afternoon, while I was in the living room of the Knudsen house, having just hung up the telephone after talking with a newspaperman, two Norwegian policemen burst into the room, seized me, and took me outside. There I saw a car filled with policemen, which had brought Trotsky from Oslo. I was unable to exchange any words with him. Wolf was in another car, into which I was pushed. A policeman had hastily fetched my suitcase from the house with my few personal belongings, and we immediately left for Oslo. All this was done without any explanation.

Erwin and I were taken to the central police building in Oslo, where we were asked to sign a declaration stating that we were leaving Norway of our own "free will." The word used was "freiwillig," since we were speaking German. Otherwise, we were told, we would be deported to Germany. Hitler's Germany. We refused. Wolf had some money on him, but I did not have a cent. In the cell he gave me a bill, which I slipped into one of my socks. We had no idea what would be done with us, and we did not know Trotsky's fate.

The next day, with no explanation, we were put on a train, flanked by two policemen. At the Swedish border the two Norwegian officers were replaced by two Swedish policemen, who stayed with us until we reached Denmark, where they handed us over to the Danish police. We arrived in Copenhagen on August 30, in the custody, not of two, but of six Danish policemen. We still did not know where we were going or what was happening elsewhere in the world. At the Copenhagen railroad station an important police official told us, very politely, that we would be taken to a hotel. We sped away in a car, squeezed between more policemen. When we entered the "hotel," it turned out to be a jail. In fact, it was a high-security jail. In the evening Erwin and I were put in separate cells. The cell was totally bare, except for a plank fastened to the wall and a blanket. All our clothes and personal belongings were taken from us overnight, and we were not even left with a handkerchief.

The next day we were taken away, still without the slightest explanation. We arrived at a pier and were led aboard a very small, old boat, the *Algarve*. The boat weighed anchor almost immediately. There were no policemen aboard, and the captain was cordial. We learned that the boat, which was a cargo ship, was empty, that it was going to Morocco to load copra oil, and that it would stop in Antwerp, where we could disembark. Later, once we were at sea, we learned over the radio that Trotsky and Natalia were going to be interned by the Norwegian government. The weather turned bad, making the empty boat pitch and roll. We arrived in Antwerp on September 2. Belgian policemen were waiting for us on the pier. Accompanied by them, we took a train for Paris. At the French border the Belgian policemen kept out of sight of the French policemen and told them nothing about us, for fear that the French police would force Wolf, who was Czechoslovakian, back into Belgium. We finally arrived in Paris. The attitude of the Scandinavian countries toward us had been provoked by Russian diplomatic pressure.

On September 2 Trotsky and Natalia had been interned by the Norwegian government in Sundby, a hamlet some twenty-five miles southwest of Oslo, near the village of Storsand. They were put on the second floor of a small house, the first floor being occupied by about twenty policemen. Trotsky was not allowed to receive visitors, the only excep-

*Erwin Wolf and Jean van Heijenoort disembarking from
the Norwegian ship* Algarve *in Antwerp, September 2, 1936.*

tion being his Norwegian lawyer, who came to see him a few times, and
Gérard Rosenthal, his Paris lawyer, who was permitted to visit him once
in October 1936. His mail was closely watched. The letters that he wrote
were either forwarded after great delay or returned to him. He could receive only short, rare messages.

In order to refute the false accusations hurled at him from Moscow,
Trotsky undertook, through his two lawyers, to institute proceedings in
two or three European countries against the official Communist publications that had reproduced the calumnies. But on October 29 a special
decree of the Norwegian government forbade an "interned alien" from
undertaking any court proceedings. Trotsky was even deprived of the
short walks that, carefully watched, he had been taking near the house.
His situation was that of a prisoner in jail, a harsh jail. In its treatment
of Trotsky, the "socialist" government of Norway stooped to ignominies
that, even in the dark days of Domène, the Doumergue government had
never descended to.

Back in Paris, I again took my place in the French Trotskyite group,
but my daily activities were soon devoted to collaborating with Liova in
refuting the false charges at the Zinoviev-Kamenev trial. After Trotsky
had been silenced by the Norwegian government, Liova started to write

a long text, which little by little took shape. I translated it into French, took charge of the printing, spurring on the printer, and corrected the proofs. The finished book, titled *Livre rouge,* was the first systematic exposure of the frameup at the Zinoviev-Kamenev trial.

In the fall of 1936 a commission of inquiry on the Moscow trial had been formed in Paris, with which Gérard Rosenthal was closely involved as a lawyer. I also worked with him. At the sessions of this commission I met Alfred and Marguerite Rosmer, André Breton, and Victor Serge. Breton was eager to help and full of good will. By the end of each meeting we had usually reached agreement on some text that had to be signed. Each person would get up and go over to sign it. Breton always entered his signature in green ink and wrote under his name, in a small hand, "writer," which surprised me.

During the fall of 1936, when I saw Liova almost daily, I began to know him better. He was working in the most difficult conditions: Moscow persecuted him, the French authorities troubled him, money was short, and his relations with Jeanne were far from satisfactory. Liova often displayed a kind of close-mouthed stubbornness, which in a masculine form was closer to the silent obstinacy of his mother than to the eloquent will power of his father. While we were chatting one day in his apartment on the Rue Lacretelle, I raised the question of the special measures that had been taken against homosexuals in the first period of Bolshevik power. "They were all spies," he retorted in a peremptory tone.

Liova always distrusted the leadership of the French Trotskyite group. Not without scorn, he generally referred to them as "the French," and in conversation he did not hesitate to say, "We Russians." In 1934 he praised the Stalinist Dimitrov for having "Bolshevik guts."

Liova's lack of confidence in the French Trotskyites perhaps cost him his life. When he fell sick with abdominal pains in February 1938, he could have turned to one of the leaders of the French Trotskyite group — Rous, Naville, or Gérard — who knew excellent doctors. Gérard's father, in particular, was a well-known Parisian doctor, who could have given the best advice and opened every door. Liova preferred to ensconce himself in a Russian clinic, which in Paris in 1938 could only have been staffed with White Russians and Stalinist agents. He adopted the ridiculously transparent pose of being a French engineer.

In two minutes, other Russians could not have failed to realise that he was Russian. The leadership of the French Trotskyite group learned of his admission to the clinic and of his operation only after a long delay. During the hours when he was deciding where to go, he was attended by Jeanne, whose honesty was above suspicion but who was possessed by a violent and passionate hostility to the leadership of the French group, and by Mark Zborowski, who is today known to have been a Stalinist spy. At this crucial moment Liova did not contact any leader of the French group. Although he was still perfectly conscious when he made up his mind to enter the Russian clinic in which he would eventually die, Zborowski could hardly have failed to strengthen him in this decision.

Gérard Rosenthal was one of the few channels through whom Trotsky was permitted to communicate with the world. In October Gérard was allowed to visit Trotsky briefly. He was also one of the very few people whom the Norwegian censor allowed, within narrow limits, to correspond with Trotsky. Liova, Gérard, and I met regularly to take care of the daily affairs, which were considerable: communicating with Trotsky, searching for a solution to the Norwegian impasse, working on the legal proceedings that Trotsky was trying to start at various places in order to refute the calumnies from Moscow, pushing the work of the commission of inquiry, and watching the situation of Liova, who had published *Livre rouge* under his own name, although he had promised the French authorities to abstain from any political action. There was no lack of problems, and from week to week, almost from day to day, important decisions had to be made, which took their toll on our nerves. One morning, for example, as the three of us sat talking around a small table in a café on the Boulevard Montparnasse, Gérard happened to use the name "Jeanne Molinier." I did not see very well how he could have expressed himself differently. The name Martin, which was Jeanne's maiden name, was never used in the organization. But when Liova heard the name uttered by Gérard, he rose abruptly, upsetting the table, shouted, "I cannot work in such conditions!" and left. In the following weeks I had to serve as intermediary between him and Gérard. All this did not make the work easier.

During the years that Liova spent in Paris, his closest collaborator was Mark Zborowski, who many years later was exposed as a G.P.U. agent.

Since Trotsky's arrival from Russia in Istanbul, a number of Stalinist agents had penetrated the ranks of the Trotskyite organization. Aside from what could be called local spies, that is, those who were recruited locally and whose activities did not go beyond the limits of a particular national group, there were a good half-dozen international agents, that is, those who were involved in the life of several sections, in the work of the International Secretariat, in the circulation of the *Bulletin of the Opposition,* and who worked with Liova, were in correspondence with Trotsky, and even visited him. The three most important international agents were the Sobolevicius brothers, Abraham and Ruvin, and Mark Zborowski. Their ways of operating would fill a whole book. But there are a number of other individuals whose activities remain shrouded in mystery.

Jakob Frank, also known as Graef, was one of these. He arrived in Prinkipo on May 29, 1929, and stayed for about five months as Trotsky's secretary. He had been recommended, apparently in good faith, by Raissa Adler, the wife of Alfred Adler, the Viennese psychotherapist. Of Russian origin, Raissa Timofeievna had known Trotsky during his stay in Vienna before World War I. When Trotsky arrived in Turkey in early 1929, she sent him a telegram of greeting and began a correspondence with him. Frank was a Lithuanian Jew, who in the spring of 1929, when Raissa Adler recommended him to Trotsky, was a member of the Australian Communist party, and up to the fall of 1927 he had worked as an economist in the Soviet commercial agency in Vienna. He did not conceal any of these facts from Trotsky, who at the time undoubtedly saw all of them as recommendations rather than reasons for suspicion. Frank left Prinkipo toward the end of October 1929.

There is doubt about Frank's role there. Among the persons who were in Prinkipo at the time and whom I later knew — Liova, Jeanne, Alfred and Marguerite Rosmer — nobody ever told me anything very definite about him. Jeanne, whom I questioned in 1958, remembered Frank well. She had never felt much sympathy for him, having found him boastful and snobbish; but of course she had suspected nothing. Trotsky, in any case, trusted Frank. On January 27, 1930, three months after Frank left Prinkipo, Trotsky wrote to a Czechoslovak Trotskyite: "Comrade Frank has been my secretary in Prinkipo for several months. You can have *full* confidence in him." In 1930, Frank wrote an article on the Russian economic situation that was published in the *Bulletin of the Opposition.* He began to display more and more sympathy for Stalinism and to drift away from the Left Opposition. Was he merely a turncoat, of whom there were many at that time? Maybe, and this was Trotsky's opinion. But it is also possible that he was an agent trained and controlled by the G.P.U. A number of indications support this hypothesis. The G.P.U. had an established custom of recruiting agents to work in Western Europe from among Russian-speaking Jews who were native to countries bordering on Russia. This was the case of the Sobolevicius brothers and of Zborowski. Frank fell within the same category.

But there are more clues. A number can be found in letters of the time. On January 13, 1930, Raymond Molinier wrote to Liova: "One Roman Well [Ruvin Sobolevicius], who claims to be on familiar terms with Frank, is asking to take direct charge of the circulation of the *Bulletin* in Germany." It is now known that Well was at that date a professional G.P.U. agent. He used Frank's name in order to offer his services to Liova. Well himself wrote to Trotsky on August 30, 1930, after having penetrated deeply into the German Trotskyite group, "I have already written you that I have proposed that Comrade Frank be co-opted into the national leadership [of the German Trotskyite group]." After leaving Prinkipo, Frank had written to Trotsky on December 17, 1929: "Roman Well from Leipzig makes a good impression. He works like a bull." They were weaving a tissue of mutual recommendations.

Kharin was working at the Soviet Embassy in Paris in 1929. He had displayed Trotskyite sympathies and apparently had acted as an intermediary between Trotsky and the Trotskyites in Moscow. Around July 1929, Trotsky sent to him from Prinkipo the whole typewritten text of the first issue of the *Bulletin of the Opposition,* so that Kharin could supervise the printing. Kharin handed the text over to the G.P.U. Though there was a copy, the printing of the first issue of the *Bulletin* was delayed. What was more grievous, original documents that had been brought out of Russia by Trotsky were also sent to Kharin so that they could be reproduced as cuts in the *Bulletin.* These documents were irretrievably lost. I heard about all this from Liova or Raymond Molinier, as I recall, and a letter from Trotsky seems to confirm it. On July 28, 1937, he wrote to Liova from Mexico: "The [Dewey] commission

wants to have the original or a certified copy of the letter that Krupskaia
sent me after Lenin's death. As far as I remember, the original of this
letter from Krupskaia, as well as some other valuable documents, were
lost in connection with the printing of the *Bulletin of the Opposition* (I
suspect that they were stolen by G.P.U. agents)." Trotsky denounced
Kharin as an *agent provocateur* in the letter that he entrusted to Blumkin in Prinkipo for the Moscow Trotskyites. Kharin is probably the
Joseph who was exposed as a Stalinist agent in the middle of 1929, but of
that I am not sure.

On June 18, 1930, Raymond Molinier wrote from Paris to Liova, who
was then in Prinkipo: "For the work in Büyük Ada and your replacement, you should seriously think of Obin. He knows German and French
well and, like you, Russian. He would be most devoted; he is active and
intelligent. His wife also types. Besides, she would not necessarily go,
and he does not make that a condition of his going." Paul Okun, also
known as Obin, was a Jew from the southern Ukraine, living as a refugee in Brussels, who had displayed Trotskyite sympathies. Though
he did not go to live in Prinkipo, he was soon intimately involved with
the work of the International Secretariat. Raymond Molinier arranged
for him to come to Paris at the beginning of December 1930. He took
the name of Mill, derived, if what I was told is correct, from the name of
the village where he was born, Milovoie. This village was about one
hundred and twenty miles east of Yanovka, Trotsky's birthplace. Although Obin did not settle in Prinkipo as a secretary to Trotsky, Raymond Molinier took him there for a visit of several weeks. I heard that
Trotsky was fond of exchanging childhood memories in Russian with
Mill. Toward the middle of 1932, Obin entered into negotiations with
the Soviet Embassy in Paris to return to Russia. He received permission
to go back and live in Kharkov, where he had relatives. Who was he—
turncoat or spy?

Abraham and Ruvin Sobolevicius were Lithuanian Jews who, under
the names of Abraham Senin and Roman Well, appeared on the scene
as members of the German Trotskyite group in Leipzig in 1929. As is
now known, they were then agents of the G.P.U., recruited and trained
in 1927. On April 26, 1930, Senin wrote to Trotsky: "You will perhaps
wonder that I am sending you this letter from Berlin. It is explained by
the fact that I am spending my two weeks' vacation with my wife, who is

a Russian Soviet citizen, a member of the party, and is employed at the [Soviet] trade commission here. In official [Communist] circles she is not known as my wife, which is the only reason that she has not yet lost her position." The facts themselves and the feigned candor with which they were presented form a striking parallel with the case of Jakob Frank.

The Sobolevicius brothers rose rapidly in the international organization. Well undertook responsibility for the circulation of the *Bulletin of the Opposition* in Germany. Liova soon came to rely on Well for the circulation of the journal in Russia itself and in the bordering countries, which was far more serious. The two brothers participated in the leadership of the German Trotskyite group and in the work of the International Secretariat. They well knew how to take advantage of factional fights in order to promote their rise. Because the people around Trotsky were anti-Navillists, Well and Senin were soon thoroughly anti-Naville. On December 2, 1930, Raymond Molinier wrote to Liova: "Roman Well has a tremendous hatred for Naville. Mill, too, now has a very great hatred for Naville."

In August 1931, Well and Senin went together to Turkey to see Trotsky. Senin also visited Trotsky in Copenhagen in November 1932. In December 1932, when disagreement and dissension were increasing in the German Trotskyite group, Well and Senin succeeded in carrying with them a part of the organization. The German group published a newspaper, *Die permanente Revolution,* and in January 1933, Well and Senin published a counterfeit issue, copying the masthead and the typographic style. This bogus issue, asking for a return to Stalinism, was reproduced, with appropriate comments, in the central newspaper of the German Communist party, *Die rote Fahne.* Thus, on the eve of Hitler's rise to power, the German Trotskyite group was in a shambles.

It is surprising that in the superheated political atmosphere of the years 1931-1932 the German Trotskyite group had made so little progress. They achieved nothing similar to the progress, however relative, of the French Trotskyites in the same kind of incendiary political situation from 1934 to 1936. In Germany, the Trotskyite group experienced stagnation, then complete disintegration. Many reasons can be cited, but it may well be that the deceitful intrigues of the Sobolevicius brothers were an important factor. In fact, Trotsky interpreted the situation thus on January 5, 1933, when he wrote to Raymond Molinier: "Well has hindered the progress of the German Opposition by bringing confusion into each slogan, each article, each action. It was very difficult to fight against him, since he would never dot his *i's* or cross his *t's*."

A remarkable description! It was all the more remarkable that Trotsky did not at the same time think that Well was a professional agent, but simply took him for a turncoat. His description, however, of Well's methods exactly fits the kind of tactics that a professional agent would adopt in such circumstances. Trotsky gave an accurate description, but drew the wrong conclusion. On January 14, 1933, for example, he wrote to the leadership of the German Trotskyite group, "Not the least of the reasons that the successes of the Left Opposition in Germany do not correspond to the situation, there is the paralyzing influence of the confused ideas and sabotaging methods of Well and Company." Again on September 26, 1933, Trotsky, in writing to Vitte, a Greek Trotskyite with whom he was having a factional fight, described Vitte's coalition as having "Wellist-Seninist elements." He still viewed Well's activities from the perspective of political factionalism rather than of professional espionage.

The Sobolevicius brothers momentarily disappeared from the scene, but in 1936, at the time of the first Moscow trial, Trotsky had an opportunity to concern himself with them once more. A few years earlier one of the defendants in the trial, Valentin Olberg, had been hanging around certain Trotskyite groups in Germany. Trotsky wrote about the situation to Liova on August 22, 1936: "This example [of Olberg] confirms the assumption that all the other witnesses for the prosecution have been recruited by the G.P.U. among those elements who ingratiated themselves abroad with the Left Opposition, or at least attempted to do so. These people either were already direct agents of the G.P.U. at that time or were young climbers who hoped for a career in the Left Opposition and who later used their betrayal of the Left Opposition in order to get ahead. And so on. There have been several such elements (for example, Mill in Paris, the brothers Well and Senin, Graef, among others)." In another letter, dated the same day, Trotsky wrote again to Liova: "It is necessary to ascertain whether the Messrs. Mill, Well, Senin, and Graef, who are familiar to us, in fact concealed themselves behind the unknown names found in the bill of indictment. Then they will all be unmasked as mere spies and agents provocateurs."

About 1935 Senin spent some time in Russia, where he helped the G.P.U. in the reprisals against relatives of Trotskyites who had already been deported. During the first months of the Spanish Civil War, Well was reported to be shuttling between Toulouse and Barcelona. Then one day in 1937 in Paris, Raymond Molinier, who had been obliged to abandon his business activities and was working as a taxi driver, saw Well, whom he knew well, entering a taxi just in front of his own. Well was in the company of four or five solidly built fellows. Molinier followed Well's taxi through the streets of Paris until it stopped at the door of the apartment building in which Liova lived in the Rue Lacretelle. Well stepped out with his companions, and Molinier could see that they entered an apartment quite near to Liova's. Molinier rushed to Liova's apartment to give him the information, but it was Zborowski who opened the door. He rebuffed Molinier, telling him: "We shall take care of that. It's our business." Of course!

Sometime between 1934 and 1936, after one of my returns to Paris from a stay with Trotsky, I found Mark Zborowski already established as a member of the French Trotskyite group and as Liova's collaborator. But I have no precise memories of my first meetings with him. Relations between members of the Trotskyite organization had their personal sides. With some, one would get on well and be friends; with others, one would simply work in common. My relations with Zborowski never took on any hint of cordiality. His sullen, frowning face and his colorless manner had little attraction for me. But I never had any special suspicions about him. Liova trusted him, saw him almost daily, worked with him, and spoke with him in Russian, their common mother tongue.

Zborowski had found his way to Liova through the French Trotskyite group. He had joined the group after presenting himself as a student with sympathies for Trotskyism. When Jeanne learned that he knew Russian, she introduced him to Liova. Zborowski used a very different technique from that of Well. The latter acted in Germany like a political leader. He adopted political positions, organized factions, contrived intrigues — all for the sake of throwing the Trotskyite group into confusion. It was that side of Well to which Trotsky referred on December 21,

1932, when he wrote to Raymond Molinier, "Well has astuteness and strength, he knew how to gain support among some workers; that is why he had to unmask himself so that the crisis could break out openly." Zborowski, in the French group, did nothing of the kind. He was rather like a mouse. He did not make himself conspicuous in any way. He always voted with the majority. One hardly noticed that he was there.

What exactly were his relations with Liova? I could only observe them at a distance. I would meet Liova without Zborowski, or Zborowski without Liova. I saw them together only once or twice. But my definite impression is that Zborowski never asked Liova a question that could provoke a political discussion of any sort or lead even to a serious conversation on a serious topic. He was obliging, always willing to fulfill the tasks with which Liova entrusted him. There was nothing you could grapple with in him, except his insignificance.

Well and Senin had unmasked themselves on the eve of Hitler's coming to power. In the political turbulence that followed, they were quickly forgotten. The move toward the new International opened up a new perspective. Eyes turned toward the future, not toward the past. After the Obin-Mill affair, Trotsky had acknowledged on October 10, 1932, that both he and Liova had made a "mistake" in entrusting great responsibility to someone whose almost sole qualification had been to speak Russian. This acknowledgment of error remained abstract, however, and with Well and Senin there was not even the acknowledgment. Trotsky and Liova simply turned their backs on the past and, one or two years later, repeated with Zborowski what had happened earlier: someone appeared who spoke Russian, he was grabbed, and soon he had charge of the circulation list of the *Bulletin* and was trusted in everything.

Trotsky, to be sure, often uttered words of caution to those around him. In the middle of 1932 I gave my passport to Raymond Molinier, who took it to Berlin and gave it to Liova, so that in case of emergency he could leave Germany with a false identity. Later in Prinkipo, I told the story to Trotsky. He got angry: "Imagine that I fall sick. They take me to the hospital in Istanbul and put me to sleep. Then I begin to speak about the passport in my sleep!" On October 10, 1935, Trotsky wrote to Liova, "The G.P.U. will do everything possible to get hold of my archives," which anticipated the theft on the Rue Michelet. But all such advice remained abstract. Just as Trotsky would fulminate against the misprints in his books but leave to others the trouble of correcting the proofs, so he acted with respect to other details. He was too lordly to attend to such matters.

Trotsky once told me that Lenin, even when he was in power, would personally address the envelopes of the letters that he sent. This reveals a care for detail that was alien to Trotsky, who always preferred to use secretaries. But even with all Lenin's mistrust, he was deceived by Malinovsky, which shows that one should use great caution in adducing personal traits to explain the events. Despite this reservation, it must be said that there was in Trotsky not only an impatience with detail but also a confidence in his own ideas, an intellectual ardor, which led him to believe that, under the proper conditions, his ideas could not fail to conquer. In the spring of 1938, for example, we were looking for a Russian typist, because Rita had left to get married and Sara Jacobs, who had come in her place, could not stay for long. We wrote to various countries, asking for help. From Czechoslovakia came the answer that a young Czech woman there who knew Russian perfectly and typed in Russian was ready to come to Mexico, the only black mark against her being that she was perhaps a Stalinist. I entered Trotsky's study to give him the news. He made a sweeping gesture with his left arm and said: "Let her come! We shall win her over!"

On May 14, 1938, Trotsky wrote to Jan Frankel, who was then in New York, about this young woman: "She is a quite young girl of eighteen. I do not believe that she can be a terrible agent of the G.P.U. Even if she comes with some sympathies for the Stalinists and with some wicked intentions against us (which I consider impossible, for nobody would entrust diabolical schemes to a little girl without experience), even in that case we feel strong enough to watch her, to control her, and to re-educate her." On June 18, 1938, Trotsky wrote again to Frankel: "If the Czech girl is a *good typist,* I would be ready to accept her immediately. The political apprehensions are in this case not very serious. A girl of eighteen years cannot make conspiracies in our home: we are stronger. In two or three months she would be totally assimilated." What confidence in his own ideas! But knowing what one does today, one trembles to read these lines. In addition, Trotsky's understanding of the psychology of eighteen-year-old girls seems rather short-sighted. Baudelaire saw deeper.

To Naville, who expressed suspicion about Zborowski, Trotsky answered one day, "You want to deprive me of my collaborators!" This was a rather strange way of looking at things. When Blumkin visited Trotsky in Prinkipo in 1929, Trotsky gave him a handwritten letter for the members of the opposition group in Moscow. Was this letter really advisable?

Even though at the time of the Barbizon affair Trotsky, in a declaration to the press, called himself, "an old conspirator," just two weeks later he was breaking the rules of conspiracy. At the end of April 1934, while he was living in a hotel in Chamonix, his relations with the French authorities were at their most critical point, for the French government was about to make a decision about his fate. Trotsky started to work on a draft of theses on the struggle against war, theses that were to be published in the name of the International Secretariat. If ever there was a document that fit the definition of conspiracy, this was it. Trotsky threw a leaf of his draft into the wastepaper basket of his hotel room, whence it found its way into the hands of a police official. All of Henri Molinier's adroitness was required to minimize the affair.

As for Liova's relations with his father, they required a measure of diplomacy. Liova would tell Trotsky about some things but kept silent on others. For example, on the night of November 6, 1936, in Paris the G.P.U. stole a part of Trotsky's archives which had been stored in an apartment on the Rue Michelet. The French police established that the burglary had been carried out with unusual professional skill, and through Zborowski the G.P.U. knew in advance what could be found at the Rue Michelet. After the burglary, however, Liova wrote to his father disingenuously that the stolen materials consisted "for the most part" of newspaper files of Trotskyite groups in various languages. It is hard to believe that the G.P.U. brought a gang of professional burglars from Moscow merely in order to steal some newspapers, knowing in advance all that they contained.

When all is said and done, Liova's blindness toward Zborowski is still astonishing. He met him almost daily for a period of several years. No language barrier stood between them. The least one can say is that Zborowski did not have an obviously revolutionary temperament. He clung to Liova, but without ever expressing any idea that one could grasp.

By December 1936, Liova and I had received confused and belated

news about the Norwegian government's plans concerning Trotsky. I
find in an old passport of mine the trace of a German transit visa, never
used, that was granted on December 22, which I may have asked for a
few days earlier, because Liova had urged me to leave immediately for
Norway in order to meet Trotsky in Oslo and accompany him to Mexico. Finally we learned that Trotsky and Natalia had sailed for Mexico
on December 19. As soon as the situation became clear, Liova asked me
to go to Mexico. The officials in the Mexican consulate in Paris, who
had received instructions on Cárdenas' orders, showed themselves to be
very obliging and immediately issued to me all the papers necessary to
enter Mexico. I did not know very much about this new country. On the
eve of my departure, in fact, I remember going to the Bibliothèque
Sainte-Geneviève to read the article on Mexico in an old encyclopedia.

4. COYOACÁN

On December 28, 1936, I boarded the *Empress of Australia* in Cherbourg, bound for New York. It was winter and the large ship was almost empty. On board was a group of American students, who were going back home after a stay of several months in Europe. It was my first contact with American young people, and I felt their vitality and spontaneity.

I spent a few days in New York, where I met some American Trotskyites. I remember in particular a dinner at James Burnham's home, where there were candles on the table, which somewhat surprised me. I stayed at the apartment of Harold Isaacs. In early January, in the midst of a snowstorm, I took a plane from Newark for Mexico City. The plane got no farther than Little Rock or Memphis before having to land. Because the blizzard was raging all over the Southwest, I traveled by railroad across the icy plains. Upon finally arriving in Laredo, I took a plane for Mexico City, landing there at midday on January 11. From the airport I took a cab for Coyoacán. In a blue house on Avenida Londres, which was surrounded by policemen, I met Trotsky and Natalia, who had arrived from Tampico an hour earlier. I gave them all the news from Paris.

Released at last from the Norwegian cage, Trotsky was in high spirits and eager to get to work. The secretarial work had to be organized as quickly as possible, in a new country with a new language. My first task was to find a Russian typist. A very competent one, Rita Jakovlevna, started to work on January 16.

The second Moscow trial, that of Radek, Piatakov, Muralov, Sokolnikov, and a dozen others, was then taking place. Each day, press releases arrived reporting the charges fabricated in Moscow, and Trotsky responded with articles exposing the mechanics of the fraud. Each article had to be immediately translated into English and Spanish, then distributed to the international news services and the Mexican newspapers.

Trotsky and Natalia disembarking in Tampico on January 9, 1937, followed by Frida Kahlo and Mexican officials.

In the evening, I made the rounds of the editorial offices of Mexico City's dailies, giving them Trotsky's statement of the day.

One of the false accusations of the second Moscow trial was that Piatakov had flown to Norway in December 1935 to meet Trotsky. Norwegian officials revealed that at that time the Oslo airport had been closed because of bad weather. On January 29, Trotsky told me, "As a raven can provoke an avalanche, the story of Piatakov's plane can be the beginning of Stalin's fall." On January 31, after Piatakov had been shot, Trotsky again observed to me, "This will cost Stalin everything." His perspective was surprisingly short. Undoubtedly he was also thinking of Stalin when on the same day he told me, "Guile is a low form of intelligence."

Diego Rivera had offered Trotsky the blue house on Avenida Londres in Coyoacán. Rivera and Frida Kahlo, his wife, were living in San Angel, two or three miles away. Diego and Frida were very attentive to Trotsky. We soon met the most active members of the Mexican Trotskyite group, who were mostly young schoolteachers or workers. Two or three of them would come every evening to mount guard through the night, so that I could rest from the day's work. A high Mexican official, Antonio Hidalgo, was the intermediary between the Mexican government and Trotsky; he quickly became a personal friend as well. He was an upright man, of great character, who had gone through the Mexican Civil War. Trotsky and Natalia became fond of him. As for me, I would run to his office whenever there was a problem to be settled with some official, and he was always ready to help.

At the beginning of February, we spent two or three days with Hidalgo in the country house of Bojórquez, near Cuernavaca. Bojórquez too was a high Mexican official. Though a friend of Hidalgo, he was more reserved toward us. Relations between Trotsky and him were courteous but nothing more. During our stay in Bojórquez' villa, we spent a day at Múgica's ranch, which was close by. Múgica's official position was Minister of Communications and Public Works, but in fact he was perhaps the closest friend and collaborator of Cárdenas, who, as the chief of state, could not possibly undertake to meet with Trotsky. The meeting with Múgica was meant in a way to substitute for it. Múgica was a man of great intelligence. With a high forehead and sparkling eyes, he had a certain physical resemblance to Trotsky, which he perhaps cultivated. During the visit, the conversation was friendly and animated. It dealt with Mexico, its economic and social problems, but did not go beyond generalities.

The American Trotskyites had called a meeting for February 16 in a large hall in New York, the Hippodrome. Trotsky was to speak by telephone from Mexico, in both Russian and English. Late in the afternoon, Trotsky, Natalia, and I were led into a small room in the premises of the telephone company in Mexico City. A microphone had been set up in the middle of the room, and an engineer had given Trotsky instructions on how he should speak. At various times over the next several hours, the connection was made with New York and Trotsky prepared to speak, but then almost immediately the circuit was broken. Finally, we had to quit. At the time I was not yet familiar with the Mexican milieu. If I had had the experience then that I acquired later, an alternative could perhaps have been found. In New York, Max Shachtman took from his pocket the English text of Trotsky's speech, sent a few days before as a precautionary measure, which he read to the audience. In 1937, telephone communication obviously did not have the quality and dependability that it has today. But we were, after all, in the telephone exchange itself, surrounded by engineers. There is hardly any

Trotsky in the patio of the house on Avenida Londres, Coyoacán, January 1937, shortly after his arrival in Mexico.

doubt in my mind that the communication was somehow sabotaged, either by Russian agents or by United States authorities.

Jan Frankel arrived from Czechoslovakia on February 19. Bernard Wolfe, a member of the American Trotskyite group, came to live in the house and work as the English secretary. It had been a long time since Trotsky had had such a secretarial staff. He was working quite hard.

Shortly after his arrival in Mexico, Trotsky had asked for the formation of an international inquiry commission that would examine the false accusations made against him and his son in the Moscow trials. The plan took a big step forward when John Dewey, the American philosopher, agreed to serve as a member of the commission and even to become its chairman. Besides six Americans, the commission included a Frenchman (Alfred Rosmer), two Germans (Otto Rühle and Wendelin Thomas), an Italian (Carlo Tresca), and a Mexican (Francisco Zamora). Suzanne La Follette was extremely active and diligent as the secretary of the commission.

In February an American writer, Waldo Frank, came to Mexico. He had personal ties with Stalinists in the United States and Latin America, but the Moscow trials had puzzled him. He sent Trotsky a letter requesting an interview, and Trotsky, before making a decision, asked me to meet Frank in the city in order to test the ground. When I met Frank in the lobby of his hotel, the first thing he said to introduce himself — knowing that I was French — was, "You understand, I am the André Gide of the Americas." He visited Trotsky twice; their conversations, though animated, led nowhere. Frank received an invitation from Dewey in New York to stay on in Mexico so as to take part in the work of the commission of inquiry when its representatives arrived, but he found a pretext to dodge the issue.

A subcommission arrived in Mexico in April to hear Trotsky's deposition and to interrogate him. The hearings took place April 10-17 in the largest room of the house on Avenida Londres. There were about forty seats for journalists and invited guests, all of which raised great security problems.

The hearings of the subcommission meant long days of work for those around Trotsky. Folders that had passed untouched through Alma Ata and Prinkipo were opened for the first time since they had left Moscow. Masses of documents had to be read, in order to find here or there some

Jean van Heijenoort, Albert Goldman, Trotsky, Natalia, and Jan Frankel during an intermission of the Dewey Commission, Coyoacán, April 1937.

useful item. Dozens of affidavits about the demonstrably false assertions made at the trials had been collected throughout the world for the commission. Many of these affidavits came from persons who had become political adversaries of Trotsky's, so that a great deal of effort was required to obtain them. These affidavits had to be not only translated but also annotated, so as to be understood by the public and, in particular, by the members of the commission. Countless minute details had to be clarified, explained, arranged. Needless to say, in all this work, there was nothing falsified, nothing hidden, no thumb pressed on the scales.

We lived for weeks in feverish activity in the house at Coyoacán. Each morning, everybody would meet in Trotsky's study for the assignment of tasks. One felt that Trotsky was once again the organizer he had been during the years of the Revolution.

Jan Frankel had charge of relations with the members of the commission and with the numerous American Trotskyites who had come to Mexico. He thus spent quite a bit of time in the city. One day Trotsky went to Frankel's room to ask him for a document, and the document was not ready. Trotsky went back to his study and slammed the door. It was a glazed door with many panes, whose putty had long since been eroded by the Mexican rains. Under the impact, the panes fell out, one after another, the crystal din of each fall reverberating throughout the house.

About the sessions of the Dewey Commission I have little to add, for the minutes have been published, along with many photographs. Toward the end of the sessions, during an intermission, Trotsky and Dewey held a conversation in the patio of the house. "If all Marxists were like you, Mr. Trotsky, I would be a Marxist," said Dewey. Whereupon Trotsky retorted, "If all liberals were like you, Mr. Dewey, I would be a liberal." The vivacity of the exchange was remarkable, but it also contained an element of diplomacy. At the time Trotsky had great respect for Dewey's resolution and character. But when Dewey a few months later, after announcing in a radio broadcast the verdict of the commission, added a few personal comments that were critical of Bolshevism, Trotsky was furious.

Hanging in the bathroom of the house, on the wall above the bathtub, was an oil painting, probably put there by Frida when she had furnished the house. The painting was a nineteenth-century Spanish nude, covered with a thick layer of dark varnish, the least naked nude that one could imagine. During the sessions of the commission, everybody—members of the commission and journalists—had to use this bathroom, the only one in the house. The day before the first session, the painting vanished, removed by Natalia at Trotsky's request. Once the sessions were over, the painting reappeared. This trifling incident indicates Trotsky's extreme distrust of newsmen and his determination not to leave himself vulnerable to slanderous gossip. But in this case he was going rather far. One can hardly imagine an American reporter, even the most ill-disposed, making a news story out of that smoky painting.

Frida was a person remarkable for her beauty, character, and intelligence. In her relations with Trotsky, she quickly adopted a certain freedom of manner. Her French was poor, but she spoke English well, having lived for quite some time in the United States while Diego was painting frescoes there. So she usually spoke with Trotsky in English, and Natalia, who could not speak English at all, found herself excluded from the conversation. Frida did not hesitate to use the word "love," after the American fashion. "All my love," she would say to Trotsky

Frida Kahlo, 1937.

upon leaving. Trotsky, who was apparently taken by Frida, began writing letters to her. He would slip a letter into a book and give the book to her, often in the presence of others, including Natalia or Diego, with the recommendation that Frida read it. I knew nothing about this little game at the time; only later did Frida tell me the story.

All this took place a few weeks after the end of the sessions of the Dewey Commission. Late in June the situation became such that those close to Trotsky began to get uneasy. Natalia was suffering. As for Diego, he had no inkling of what was going on. Since he was morbidly jealous, the least suspicion would have caused an explosion. There would have been a scandal, with grave political repercussions. Jan Frankel, as I remember, ventured to speak to Trotsky about the dangers inherent in the situation.

At the beginning of July, in order to reduce the tension that was building between them, Trotsky and Natalia decided to live apart for a time. On July 7 Trotsky went to live in the hacienda of a landlord, Landero, who was an acquaintance of Antonio Hidalgo and Diego. His hacienda was situated near San Miguel Regla, some ninety miles northeast of Mexico City, beyond Pachuca, where Trotsky could fish and ride horseback. He was accompanied there by Jesús Casas, the police lieutenant who headed the small garrison stationed at the Avenida Londres, and by Sixto, one of Diego Rivera's two chauffeurs. Natalia remained in Coyoacán.

On July 11 Frida went to see Trotsky at the hacienda. I am inclined to believe that it was at the close of this visit that Trotsky and Frida decided to put an end to their amorous relations. Till then, they had let themselves glide down the slippery path of flirtation. Now, in view of the circumstances, it was impossible for them to go further without committing themselves completely. The stakes were too high. The two partners drew back. Frida was still very much attached to Diego, and Trotsky to Natalia. Moreover, the consequences of a scandal would have been serious and far-reaching.

Natalia, who had learned about Frida's trip to the hacienda, wrote to Trotsky asking for an explanation. Trotsky, who had just done what he considered to be his duty in breaking with Frida, answered Natalia that her questions were "stupid, pitiful, self-serving." But he also called her "his victim" and declared that he was shedding tears "of pity, of repentance and of . . . torment." Thus began a series of letters that were exchanged by Trotsky and Natalia during the three weeks of their separation.

Having broken with Frida, Trotsky felt all his tenderness for Natalia returning, and the letters that he then wrote give proof of his affection for her. But they also reveal, in counterpoint, a more somber motif, involving the "torment." Through a familiar psychological mechanism, Trotsky, to lessen his feelings of guilt toward Natalia, proceeded to reproach her for an alleged infidelity. He perhaps thought that the best defense was attack. The subject was first broached rather hesitantly: "It is with shame, it is with hatred toward myself, that I write this to you." Then the tone became more strident. Trotsky asked Natalia questions about her relations with a young assistant with whom she had worked in the People's Commissariat of Public Instruction at the very beginning of the Bolshevik government, that is, twenty years earlier; the assistant had fallen in love with Natalia, but she had not responded in any way to his advances. The most violent explosion occurred, not in a letter, but by telephone, when on July 21 Trotsky called Natalia from Pachuca to give vent to his jealousy. He shouted in Russian over a defective Mexican telephone, berating her for her fictitious infidelity of two decades before. Natalia was physically shaken. "My little Leon does not trust me. He has lost confidence in me . . . It is your pride," she wrote to Trotsky immediately after the call. After his outburst over the telephone, Trotsky felt relieved and wrote to Natalia: "I think I have calmed down. In any case, I can wait till we meet again."

This attack of jealousy was apparently not an isolated incident. Trotsky himself speaks in his letters of a "recurrence," and he seemed to regard his "torment" as a kind of fever whose bouts would periodically recur. When he first met Natalia in Paris in 1903, she had a lover and felt some hesitation about leaving him. After Trotsky's death, she confided to a friend, "He never forgave me. It always kept coming up again."

During these weeks of July 1937, Natalia inadvertently dealt a severe blow to Trotsky. On July 18 she wrote him, "Everyone, at heart, is terribly alone." This remark, as she herself noted, was rather banal, but Trotsky was shaken up by it. He wrote to her, "This sentence has been a stab in my heart." There are two possible reasons for his reaction, one particular and the other general. First, the sentence betrayed a feeling of isolation on Natalia's part. Second, it violated Trotsky's conception of the communist man.

Finally, the letters exchanged by Trotsky and Natalia show, in the midst of their emotional torment, a resurgence of sexual desire. On July 19 Trotsky reported to Natalia on the condition of his penis, using a popular Russian word, and described, in the crudest language, the details of sex play that he dreamed of engaging in with her.

Trotsky came back to Coyoacán on July 26 or 27. I had entered the French hospital in Mexico City on July 17 to have my appendix removed, so I was probably not at home on Avenida Londres when Trotsky returned, or if I was, I was confined to my room. Life in the house resumed its customary course. To an outside observer, the relations among these four persons—Trotsky, Natalia, Diego, and Frida—were marked by only subtle changes. A distance had been established between Trotsky and Frida; the word "love" was heard no more. The most noticeable difference was perhaps in Natalia's attitude toward Frida, which alternated between periods of coldness and sudden demonstrations of affection. Trotsky asked Frida to give him back the letters that he had written to her, explaining, "They could fall into the hands of the G.P.U.." She returned them to him, and he apparently destroyed them. It was at this time that Frida told me about what had happened.

Trotsky's love affair with Frida was, I am certain, the first adventure of this kind that he had engaged in since leaving Russia. In Turkey, France, and Norway, circumstances did not permit such flings. Shortly after his affair with Frida, Trotsky undertook to enter into a love relation of a different character with another young woman, which I will deal with in a moment. In light of what I saw in Mexico—in the manner in which Trotsky behaved toward Frida and this other young woman and in the boldness and ease with which he conducted these enterprises —I am inclined to believe that he had had a number of affairs in the course of his life. In 1920, while Clare Sheridan was modeling a portrait bust of Trotsky in his office in the Kremlin, there had been an element of flirtation in Trotsky's conversation with her and in his general attitude toward her. I also heard, though from someone who had never known Trotsky personally, that at the time of the October insurrection Trotsky was having an affair with a young, blond Englishwoman. But I

Natalia and Trotsky in the patio of the house in Coyoacán, 1937.

have never been able to learn anything more precise about this rumor.

Bernard Wolfe went back to the United States in August. At the end of September a new American, Joseph Hansen, arrived. On the day of his arrival, or perhaps the day after, we had to pay a visit to the Fernández family, who lived in a suburb of Mexico City; three of their sons were members of the Mexican Trotskyite group. All the members of the family felt a great affection for Trotsky and Natalia, and Trotsky was fond of their company. So we drove off, Joe at the wheel, I next to him on the front seat, and Trotsky and Natalia in back. Because Joe did not know the streets of Mexico City, I gave him directions. At each intersection I would say "Left," "Right," or "Straight ahead." The day after this visit, we for some reason had to go back to the Fernández home, although two visits in two days was rather unusual. Because the trip was long and complicated, it was unthinkable that Joe would remember the way, so as on the previous day, I guided him: "Left," "Right," "Straight ahead." After we had returned to Coyoacán, Trotsky asked me to come to his study. "Don't you think that we should send Joe back to the United States?" he asked. I was surprised. "He will never learn!" Trotsky exclaimed. I pleaded Joe's cause, trying to explain the difficulties involved. Without showing any sign of belief, Trotsky replied, "We shall see!" As it turned out, in fact, of all the Americans who lived in Coyoacán, Joe was the one with whom Trotsky got along best and for whom he developed the most esteem.

At the end of October, Jan Frankel left for the United States. At the beginning of November Gaby arrived from France with our son. Although she was a member of the Molinier group in France, she had agreed while in Mexico not to engage in any political activity. Once settled in Coyoacán, she began to help Natalia with the daily chores, just as she had in Barbizon.

One day a few weeks after her arrival, Gaby was preparing lunch in the kitchen with Natalia and a young Mexican maid. At that time, Natalia's Spanish was poor; she in fact knew hardly any words. She made herself understood by gestures and single words, often pulling a maid by the arm to make her see something. On this particular morning, for some reason Gaby thought that Natalia was treating the Mexican maid harshly, and she told her so. Gaby had a frank way of speaking that was common to Belleville, the district in Paris where she had lived most of her life. Also, her membership in the Molinier group had imbued her with a certain animosity toward the Trotskys, which now spilled out. Finally, the thing that often happens when two people are working together in a kitchen happened now: voices were raised. At this point, Trotsky passed by the kitchen on the way from his study to the bathroom. He heard the voices raised in anger, entered the kitchen, saw the scene, and shouted, "I am going to call the police!" Although he did nothing of the sort, disastrous words had nevertheless been spoken.

On the afternoon of the same day, while I was alone sorting papers, Trotsky came to see me. "I should not have said that," he admitted in a confused, almost sheepish manner. This was the only time that I ever saw him so embarrassed. In any case, Gaby could not stay in the house. She went back to France with our son, via New York.

On November 12, 1937, Trotsky asked me to send the following cable:

CHAUTEMPS PREMIER PARIS

  REGARDING ASSASSINATION IGNAZ REISS THEFT MY ARCHIVES AND SIMILAR CRIMES I INSIST NECESSITY SUBJECTING TO INTERROGATION AT LEAST AS WITNESS JACQUES DUCLOS VICECHAIRMAN CHAMBER DEPUTIES OLD GPU AGENT

TROTSKY

The word "old" obviously meant that Trotsky had known about Duclos' connection with the G.P.U. while Trotsky was still a member of the Soviet government; thus he was revealing a state secret. The cable caused a turmoil in the Trotskyite ranks. Liova, in particular, thought that his father had made an error in sending it.

Several times during the year 1937 we had received letters from Naville telling us that André Gide intended to come to Mexico; each time, however, he postponed his departure. In November, Gide's plan seemed to have become more definite. Trotsky tried to conquer his last hesitations. For a while he thought of writing Gide to tell him how much Mexico had to offer him, but he refrained from doing so because, he thought, Gide might regard such a letter as an attempt to maneuver him. Proceeding less directly, Trotsky wrote the draft of a letter, which began "Dear Master" and detailed all the things that could induce Gide o. The letter was to be signed by several Mexican artists ng them Diego Rivera, Salvador Novo, and Carlos Pellicer. I do not remember whether the letter was actually sent; but if it was, it was of no avail, for we soon learned that Gide had suddenly changed his plans and left for Africa.

The house on Avenida Londres, with its patio, two courtyards, and outbuildings, formed a perfect rectangle. Two opposite sides of this rectangle were situated on two parallel streets, Avenida Londres and Avenida Berlin. The third side abutted a street perpendicular to these two, Calle Allende. All windows facing on these three streets had been blocked in with adobe bricks. The fourth side of the property formed the boundary with another property. All along this side ran a high wall, which was a drawback rather than an advantage because we could not observe what was happening on the other side. Besides, the wall was close to the bedroom of Trotsky and Natalia. This layout was a constant source of worry for Diego Rivera and myself, and we spoke about it often.

Trotsky's concern lay in another direction. By the end of 1937, the campaign of insults and threats conducted against him by the Mexican Stalinists was becoming more and more vicious. Trotsky envisaged the possibility of a frontal attack against the house, launched by a few hundred persons on the corner of Avenida Londres and Calle Allende. The attack could be disguised as a political demonstration and could end in an attempt on his life. One day he described to me his plan of defense, which was to have a ladder always available at the foot of the wall in the extreme corner of the second courtyard, on Avenida Berlin. This street, which at that time was covered with grass, was hardly ever used, and at night it was poorly lighted, or perhaps not at all. From the outside it was not clear that our property extended so far. In case of an attack, Trotsky would put the ladder against the wall, cross over alone and unseen, and quickly walk to the house of a young Mexican woman whom we knew, to take refuge there. The woman lived in her own home a few blocks from the blue house. The climb over the wall had merit. It in fact was a clever plan, which appealed to me. Sometime later, Trotsky proposed to me that we have a rehearsal. He would put his ladder against the wall in the evening and go to the house of the young woman. But meanwhile I had learned from her that, over the last two or three months, Trotsky had made her four or five direct and pressing propositions, which she had simply ignored without making any fuss. In particular, Trotsky had revealed to her the plan of the ladder and the prospect of a rehearsal. The whole affair thus took on a different aspect. This combination of security procedures with an amorous adventure hardly pleased me. Although I said nothing to Trotsky, he may have noted my lack of enthusiasm, because he did not insist on the rehearsal. Besides, the situation soon took a new turn.

Various signs, certain comings and goings, made the neighboring house appear more and more suspect to both Diego Rivera and myself. Giving proof of his great generosity, Rivera decided to buy it. The transaction, however, would take a few weeks. These weeks were dangerous ones, because, if an attempt on Trotsky's life were really in preparation, the agents would hasten to execute it before losing the house. The plan that we finally adopted was for Trotsky to go to live, until we could take possession of the neighboring house, at the home of Antonio Hidalgo in Lomas de Chapultepec, a fashionable district of Mexico City. In the meantime, everything would be done to conceal Trotsky's absence from the house in Coyoacán.

So on February 13, 1938, Trotsky slipped into the car, which was parked in the rear courtyard, and lay down on the floor. I took the wheel and the gate was opened. I sped out past the policemen's booth, waving to them familiarly, just as I always did when leaving alone in a hurry. Trotsky then got up and sat on the back seat, where he remained until we arrived at Hidalgo's home.

The house was very comfortable. As there were no children, Hidalgo and his wife showered their attention on Trotsky, who spent his time reading and writing. Back in Coyoacán, Natalia had arranged pillows in the bed to simulate Trotsky's body, as Alexandra Lvovna had done thirty-five years earlier when Trotsky had escaped from Siberia. The servants were kept away from the room, and from time to time Natalia would get some tea from the kitchen for an allegedly sick Trotsky. Communications between Coyoacán and Chapultepec were conducted through either Hidalgo or me.

This was the situation when, on February 16, news came of Liova's death. Because of the time difference, the news arrived in Coyoacán at the end of lunch. It was given to us over the telephone by, I think, one of the representatives of a big American press agency. Joe Hansen and Rae Spiegel were with me in the house. We decided not to tell anything to

Natalia, nor to let her see the afternoon newspapers or to come to the telephone. I immediately left to see Rivera at his house in San Angel. While there, we may have had a telephone conversation with somebody in Paris, perhaps Gérard Rosenthal or Jean Rous. Then Rivera and I left for Chapultepec.

As soon as we entered the room where Trotsky was, Rivera stepped forward and told him the news directly. Trotsky, his face hardening, asked, "Does Natalia know?" To Rivera's negative answer, he replied, "I shall tell her myself!" We left at once. I drove, with Rivera at my side. Trotsky sat in the back, stiff and silent. Upon arriving in Coyoacán, he immediately shut himself up with Natalia in their room. Once again they secluded themselves as they had in Prinkipo at the time of Zina's death. Through the half-opened door, tea was passed to them. On February 18 at one o'clock in the afternoon, Trotsky handed me a few sheets of paper, handwritten with notes in Russian, which he asked me to translate and distribute to the reporters. In these lines he asked for an investigation of the circumstances of his son's death. When, after a few days of confinement, Trotsky reappeared in his study, he started to write an article about Leon Sedov (Liova). Shortly before moving to Hidalgo's house, he had finished a long article, "Their Morals and Ours," which he had dated February 10, 1938. After Liova's death, he changed the date to February 16 and added a postscript.

Immediately after Liova's death Jeanne, who had become very attached to him, wrote letters to Trotsky and Natalia full of despair. Trotsky sent her a consoling telegram: "Yes, little Jeanne, we must live." But the situation soon changed. At the time of his death, Liova had left many papers in his apartment on the Rue Lacretelle, and two or three weeks afterward it became apparent that Jeanne, who belonged to the Molinier group, was not inclined to forward these papers to Trotsky through the agency of Gérard Rosenthal, Trotsky's lawyer in Paris, who belonged to the official French Trotskyite group. Trotsky bristled with anger. The papers, he felt, belonged to him, both legally and morally. He also thought that Jeanne was playing with fire, because the French police were only looking for a pretext to poke their noses into the papers, as was the G.P.U. too. He became furious. A series of bitter and harrowing squabbles began. Meanwhile, Natalia kept up a friendly correspondence with Jeanne, and the two heartbroken women continued to exchange tearful letters.

About six weeks after Liova's death, at the end of March or beginning of April, after lunch while Trotsky was having his siesta I was in my room. It was the time of day when Natalia would often come to my room to speak of minor problems in the household or to go over accounts. As she entered the room on this day, she was very agitated. Tears ran down her cheeks. She cried out: "Van, Van, you know what he told me? 'You are with my enemies!' " And she repeated the sentence in Russian, using Trotsky's own words. He had not said "adversaries," but "enemies." And his enemies at this time, while they began with Jeanne and Raymond Molinier, went much further. The sentence, of course, could be interpreted, "You are acting as if you were with my enemies" or "You are playing into the hand of my enemies." But the harsh fact remains that, six weeks after Liova's death, while Natalia was still devastated with grief, Trotsky had spoken to her in the most cutting and brutal terms possible.

Around that time we learned that André Breton was coming to Mexico to give some conferences, sent by the French Ministry of Foreign Affairs. Trotsky asked me to get him some of Breton's books, none of which he had ever read. As time was short, I decided to write to New York rather than Paris. On April 9 I mailed a letter to Harold Isaacs, asking him to send us all the books by Breton that he could find in the city. At the end of April the *Manifeste du surréalisme, Nadja, Les vases communicants,* and one or two more arrived. I cut the pages of those that were new and brought the books to Trotsky. He stacked them on the far corner of his desk, where they remained for several weeks. My impression is that he leafed through them but certainly did not read them from beginning to end.

As soon as Breton and his wife Jacqueline reached Mexico City, in the second half of April, I went to see them in town. We had lunch in a typical Mexican restaurant. Breton seemed delighted to be in Mexico; everything was a marvel to him. He was very cordial to me. On April 29, 1938, I wrote to Pierre Naville: "Breton has been here for a few days, full of admiration for the country, for Diego's paintings, for all the beautiful things in this country. On the other hand, he goes from banquets to official receptions, he is beset by a multitude of people." A few days later I went to fetch Breton and Jacqueline from Mexico City and bring them to Coyoacán. At this first meeting with Trotsky and Natalia, the talk ran on the work of the commission of inquiry on the Moscow

trials in Paris, on Gide's attitude toward the trials, on Malraux's attitude. News was exchanged, but no major topic was approached. The
second meeting took place a few days later, on May 20. I have kept a few
notes, written immediately after the meeting for my personal use. These
notes are in no sense minutes, but they do give some indication of what
happened. As soon as Breton, Jacqueline, Natalia, and I were seated in
Trotsky's study, Trotsky promptly launched into a defense of Zola. He
interpreted surrealism as a reaction against realism or naturalism, in
Zola's narrow and specific literary sense of realism. He said: "When I
read Zola, I discover new things, things that I did not know. I enter into
a broader reality. The fantastic is the unknown." Breton, taken aback,
stiffened. Sitting bolt upright against the back of his chair, he replied:
"Yes, yes, I agree. There is poetry in Zola." Trotsky went on: "You in-
voke Freud, but does he not do the opposite? Freud raises the subcon-
scious into the conscious. Are you not trying to smother the conscious
under the unconscious?" Breton answered, "No, no, obviously not."
Then he asked the inevitable question: "Is Freud compatible with
Marx?" Trotsky answered: "Oh, you know! These are questions that
Marx did not study. For Freud, society is an absolute, except perhaps in
The Future of an Illusion, and it takes the abstract form of coercion.
One would have to enter into an analysis of society itself."

The conversation took on a lighter tone when Natalia served tea.
Talk turned to the relations between art and politics. Trotsky posed the
idea of an international federation of revolutionary artists and writers,
to counterbalance the Stalinist organizations. It was clear that he had
held such a plan in mind since hearing about Breton's anticipated trip
to Mexico. The prospect of a manifesto was mentioned. Breton agreed
to submit a draft.

In the following weeks there were no further meetings in Trotsky's
study, but they took excursions together, including picnics in the Mexican countryside. Breton and Jacqueline were in daily contact with Rivera and Frida. They even lived for a time in Rivera's house in San
Angel, and when they had first arrived in Mexico, they were sheltered
by Guadalupe Marin, one of Diego Rivera's former wives, in her Mexico
City apartment. But with Trotsky, there were perhaps only eight or ten
meetings altogether.

Breton's trip to Mexico had provoked angry reactions on the part of

Trotsky (seated), Diego Rivera, Natalia, Reba Hansen,
André Breton, Frida Kahlo, and Jean van Heijenoort
on an outing near Mexico City, June 1938.

Diego Rivera, Frida Kahlo, Natalia, Reba Hansen, André Breton,
Trotsky, an unidentified Mexican, Jesús Casas (head of the police
garrison protecting Trotsky), Sixto (one of Rivera's two chauffeurs),
and Jean van Heijenoort on an outing in Chapultepec, June 1938.

the Stalinists. Breton himself spoke of their venomous plots in a speech of November 11, 1938, after his return to Paris. Breton's first conference in Mexico was scheduled to take place in the Palacio de Bellas Artes. Trotsky was worried that a gang of Mexican Stalinists might very well disrupt the meeting by violence. He asked me to organize a discrete security force. I came to an agreement with members of the Mexican Trotskyite group that they would station themselves at a number of strategic spots without attracting attention. Nothing untoward happened. But the fact that Trotsky did not hesitate to call upon the members of a political group in order to guarantee the security of a literary conference by Breton shows, in my opinion, the extent of his goodwill toward Breton.

One afternoon, during one of our excursions with Breton and Jacque-

line, we stopped in a small town to visit a church. It was near Puebla
and may have been Cholula. Neither Rivera nor Frida was with us. The
inside of the church was low and dark. On the left, the wall and pillars
were covered with the votive offerings that are peculiar to Mexico.
These are small metal plates, sometimes made out of old cans, on which
popular artists have painted dramatic scenes, generally of grave acci-
dents, from whose fatal consequences the one who is offering the painting has been saved by divine providence. The offering is hung as a token
of thanks. As these offerings are left to accumulate, some are more than
eighty years old. They are, in my view, the most remarkable form of
popular art in Mexico. Breton was filled with admiration. So filled that
he started to slip some of the votive offerings, perhaps half a dozen,
under his jacket. He felt even fewer scruples by virtue of the fact that it
was a church, and he perhaps even considered his act to be a legitimate
expression of anticlericalism.

Trotsky was furious, as I could see immediately from his face. This
was not his kind of anticlericalism. The situation, moreover, held a danger for him. In Mexico, all church property belongs to the state. If the
local authorities had become aware of the theft, it would have caused a
scandal, which the Stalinists, then so fiercely eager to compromise Trotsky's stay in Mexico, would have seized upon. Playing upon Mexican
patriotism, they could have accused Trotsky and his friends of striking
at the Mexican heritage. The consequences might have been very serious. Trotsky walked out of the church without saying a word. I must
admit that on this occasion he showed great self-control.

Soon afterward, Trotsky began to press Breton for the draft of the
manifesto. Breton, with Trotsky breathing down the back of his neck,
felt completely paralyzed, unable to write, which was quite understand-
able. "Have you something to show me?", Trotsky would ask whenever
they met. As the situation developed, Trotsky assumed the role of the
schoolmaster before a Breton playing the recalcitrant pupil who had not
done his homework. Although Breton was keenly embarrassed, the situation dragged on. One day in the garden at Diego Rivera's house, he
took me aside to ask me, "Why don't you write this manifesto?" I de-
clined, not wanting to muddle the affair still more.

In June we left on a trip to Guadalajara. Diego Rivera was already
there, painting, and we were supposed to join him. We drove in two

cars. In the first car, driven, I believe, by Joe Hansen, were Trotsky and Natalia, seated in back, and next to the driver, Breton, whom Trotsky had asked to travel with him so that they could talk. I was in the second car with Jacqueline, perhaps Frida, and an American or Mexican driver. After about two hours of driving, during a trip that at the time took about eight hours, the first car stopped. We stopped also, some fifty yards behind, and I walked up to the first car to see what was going on. Joe came toward me, saying, "The old man wants you." Meanwhile, Breton had gotten out of the first car and was walking toward the second one. As we passed, without saying a word, he made a gesture of baffled astonishment. I got into the first car, and we started off. Trotsky remained in the back, upright and silent. He gave me no explanation of what had happened.

When we arrived in Guadalajara, we went to a hotel, without making contact with the Breton-Rivera group. I was perplexed. Joe, who did not know French, had been unable to follow the conversation between Trotsky and Breton, so he could give me no information. Natalia was rather vague about it. Once settled down, the first thing that Trotsky asked me to do was to arrange a meeting with Orozco, who was then living in Guadalajara. Rivera and Orozco were the two most famous Mexican painters of the day. Although they were not personal enemies, in character, tastes, ways of life, and styles of painting, they were at opposite poles. Orozco was as tormented an introvert as Rivera was a hearty extrovert. The mere fact of their being the two greatest painters in the country was bound to create a rivalry between them, and they had hardly any personal contact. What Trotsky was asking of me was clear; he wanted to establish a distance from the Rivera-Breton group.

I went to see Orozco, who received me in his studio, and we arranged a meeting. On the next day or so, Trotsky, Natalia, and I visited him. The conversation was pleasant, but it certainly did not have the briskness and warmth that generally characterized conversations between Trotsky and Rivera. Upon leaving, Trotsky told Natalia and me, "He is a Dostoevsky!" Meanwhile, Rivera and Breton were wandering around Guadalajara, looking for paintings and old objects.

We started back to Mexico City, without Trotsky's having seen Breton again. Trotsky's wrath on the road to Guadalajara had been provoked by Breton's persistent delay in not coming up with the draft of the manifesto. But apparently Trotsky had regained his self-control and did not want a break, for once everybody was home from Guadalajara, relations were reestablished little by little. Breton never told me in detail what had happened in the car, and I did not ask him.

At the beginning of July, it was decided to spend a few days in Pátzcuaro, in the state of Michoacán. Breton, Jacqueline, and I left ahead, for I was to find a suitable hotel for Trotsky, and Breton and Jacqueline wanted to see the countryside. Diego Rivera had a large collection of pre-Columbian figurines from Chupicuaro in his house in San Angel, which had been brought to him a few at a time by peasants from the state of Guanajuato. These clay figurines, some three inches high, represented naked women, adorned and voluptuous. Their almond eyes and sexual organs were made of small pieces of added clay. Breton had greatly admired these ladies of Chupicuaro. Near Morelia, Breton asked me whether we could make a detour and try to find some of the figurines in a village. We would have to improvise, because we had no exact information, but we went on a gamble. As we drove down a dirt road, in the middle of the rainy season, the car got stuck. We called to some peasants for help, and after a great effort they were able to pull us out of an awkward situation. We abandoned our plan to look for the ladies of Chupicuaro and returned to the road to Pátzcuaro. When we were on our way, Breton remarked to me, "If I had been alone, quite simply I would have left everything there and continued on foot." That seemed strange to me. Where would he have gone, in the middle of the fields of Mexico?

Once in Pátzcuaro, we took a boat ride on the lake and, at nightfall, ate *pescado blanco* on the small island of Janitzio. The little town of Pátzcuaro was then quiet and charming. Walking down its cobblestone streets or through its quiet squares, one would have thought it to be the seventeenth century. The hotel that we selected was in fact a large old house, with perhaps ten rooms and a garden full of flowers. About two days after we had settled in, Trotsky arrived with Natalia and two Americans, one of whom was, I believe, Joe Hansen. Diego Rivera and Frida also arrived. Plans were made. After excursions during the day, there were to be evening conversations about art and politics. There was even a plan afoot to publish these talks under the title "Conversations in Pátzcuaro," with Breton, Rivera, and Trotsky as authors. On the first

evening Trotsky did most of the talking. He developed the thesis that in
the communist society of the future, art would dissolve into life. There
would be no more dances or dancers, but everybody would move har-
moniously. There would be no more paintings, but houses would be
decorated. Discussion of this thesis was put off until the next evening,
and Trotsky retired early, as was his custom. I stayed chatting with Breton in the garden. "Don't you think that there always will be people who
will want to paint a small square of canvas?" he asked me.

The next evening's discussion never took place, because Breton fell ill
with fever and an attack of aphasia. Jacqueline took care of him with
great devotion. We were disturbed, but she told us that it had occurred
before.

On July 10 a group of schoolteachers from neighboring villages, having learned that Trotsky was in Pátzcuaro, came to talk with him. The
conversation centered upon the tasks and problems of a schoolteacher in
a village. Trotsky compared Mexico to Russia. At the end of the conversation, he penciled a short note in Russian on the topic. I translated it
into Spanish, and the text was given to the visitors, to be published in a
small newspaper, *Vida,* the schoolteachers' organ in Michoacán. Shortly
thereafter we left Breton to the care of Jacqueline, and the rest of the
household returned to Coyoacán.

After a few days, Breton and Jacqueline reappeared. Breton had re-
covered rather quickly. From the blind alley that the manifesto draft
had become, a way out was finally found. If I remember correctly, Breton took the first step. He gave Trotsky a few sheets of paper, covered
with his tiny handwriting. Trotsky dictated a few pages in Russian, to be
combined with Breton's text. I translated Trotsky's pages into French
and then showed them to Breton. After more talk, Trotsky took all of
the texts, cut them, added a few passages, and pasted everything into a
long roll. I typed the resulting text in French, translating Trotsky's Russian and keeping Breton's prose. This was the text on which they reached
final agreement. Whoever reads it can, from the language, unerringly
recognize the paragraphs written by Trotsky and those written by Breton. Trotsky wrote a bit less than half the text, Breton a bit more. Directed to artists, the manifesto was published over the signatures of Breton and Rivera, although Rivera had taken no part in its writing. The
manifesto called for the creation of an International Federation of Inde-

pendent Revolutionary Artists (I.F.I.R.A.). It was translated into several languages and became well known.

The last meeting between Trotsky and Breton, just before Breton's departure for France, was cordial and warm. War threatened, and Breton expected to be drafted on his arrival in France. The parting came at the end of July 1938, on the sun-drenched patio of the blue house in Coyoacán, amidst cactus, orange trees, bougainvilleaes, and idols. Trotsky went to his study and returned, carrying the joint manuscript of the manifesto. He gave it to Breton, who was very moved. On Trotsky's part this was an unusual gesture, which I never saw repeated during all the time that I was with him. The manuscript must still be in the papers left by Breton.

Back in France, Breton was drafted, as we had feared, but for a few weeks only. On November 11, 1938, he delivered a stirring speech describing his stay in Mexico. In referring to me in this speech, Breton incidentally said that I was "very poor." The categories of "poor" and "rich" were not ones in which I ever thought of placing myself during my life with Trotsky. Obviously there was little money in the house, I did not have what could be called a salary, and small personal expenses were taken care of in the simplest way between Natalia and myself. But when I brought the printed text of Breton's speech to Trotsky in his study, I was rather embarrassed, fearing that he would think that Breton's remark had been provoked by some complaint on my part. He said nothing, I said nothing, and there never was any misunderstanding between us on that score. What Breton's remark indicates, nevertheless, is that Surrealists and Trotskyites were living in different worlds.

Breton's visit had not interrupted revolutionary politics. The founding conference of the Fourth International was then being prepared. On July 18 we got the news that Rudolf Klement, who was in charge of all administrative work of the International Secretariat, had disappeared. A few days later his beheaded body was found floating in the Seine. Through Zborowski, the G.P.U. knew all about Klement's activities, and it had struck when the plans for founding the Fourth International were just getting under way. The conference nevertheless took place at the beginning of September, near Paris.

Like Marx, who, when at one time confronted with some unexpected statements of his disciples, had said that he was not a "Marxist," Trotsky would at times say that he was not a "Trotskyite." In fact, he was a thoroughgoing "Trotskyite" if that term is understood to mean that he was constantly preoccupied with the internal problems of the various Trotskyite groups. Most of the time, each of these groups was divided into two or three factions. The fights between factions, their alliances and their ruptures, either within a group or from one group to another, preoccupied Trotsky, who devoted to them much of his time, energy, and patience.

Trotsky's perpetual grievance against the Trotskyite group was their poor social composition: too many intellectuals, too few workers. "Petty bourgeois" was the accusation continually hurled from his pen against persons and groups. The only two Trotskyite groups about which I heard him express unqualified admiration were the Charleroi group in Belgium, made up of coal miners, and the Minneapolis group in the United States, made up of teamsters.

To reconstruct the details of all these internal fights in the various national sections of the Trotskyite organization would be a complex and arduous task. Yet only a detailed and factual study, which would document the specific conditions of each situation, would enable one to pass judgment on Trotsky's decisions in these matters. It is too easy in this area to allow oneself superficial judgments. On the surface, the apparent result of the tremendous efforts that Trotsky devoted to organizational questions was rather meager. To take one example, Trotsky wrote pages and pages full of revolutionary passion on the subject of Spain, but during the Civil War the Trotskyite group in Barcelona numbered hardly more than a dozen members, and these were young people without great experience. At the time of Trotsky's death, the Trotskyite groups were not so different in size from the various opposition groups that he had found when he left Russia. Quite a few outstanding men had proclaimed themselves Trotskyites at one time or another, only to move away subsequently from the Trotskyite organization. But one reason for our small numbers was surely the difficulties of those dreadful years. Today it is not easy to bring the thirties to life again for those who have not known them. Stalinist slanders and persecutions were rife. Money was lacking to a degree that today is hard to imagine; for want of money, we were often paralyzed in the face of the simplest tasks.

Undoubtably, Trotsky gave most of his attention to the development of Trotskyism in France. A few months after his arrival in Turkey, he oversaw the beginnings of *La Vérité*. From 1929 to 1931, the disagreements between Raymond Molinier, Pierre Naville, and Alfred Rosmer took up a great deal of his time. From 1935 to his death, the quarrel with Raymond Molinier grew more and more bitter, until it became a nightmare. During the strikes of June 1936, he had written jubilantly, "The French revolution has begun." But then, after the defeat of the French workers and his own move to Mexico, Trotsky began to look at the problems of Trotskyism in France from a certain distance. Although he still followed what was happening on the French political scene as well as inside the French Trotskyite group, it was not with the same sustained commitment as before.

In Coyoacán, news about the internal life of the French Trotskyite group and, in particular, about the functioning of its leadership came to us mostly through Jean Rous. He wrote long letters fairly regularly, which, though intended for Trotsky, were sent in my name. Rous had a rather poor hand, and Trotsky had trouble deciphering his handwriting, so it came about that I would type each letter from Rous and then give the typewritten text to Trotsky. One day, probably in the middle of 1939, after a letter from Rous had arrived, I gave the gist of it to Trotsky in a few words and added, "I am going to type it for you." Trotsky replied: "It is not worthwhile. You have other things to do." Such an attitude would have been unthinkable a few years earlier.

An American university professor, Hubert Herring, who organized seminars in Mexico, would bring a group of perhaps thirty persons to Coyoacán once or twice a year. As part of the seminar, Trotsky would speak to them for an hour or two and answer their questions. In exchange, Herring had put at Trotsky's disposal a house that he owned in Taxco. We went there every two or three months for a week or so. The first time we did so was shortly after the end of the sessions of the Dewey Commission. In 1938, during one of our later stays in Taxo, we rented some horses for an excursion into the hills that surround the town. Accompanying us on the ride were several American Trotskyites, including a few women, who were spending two or three weeks in Mexico and had come to see Trotsky. Altogether there were over a dozen persons. We started out at a walk and it did not seem that we would ever go any faster. Suddenly, without saying a word, not even to Natalia, Trotsky whipped up his horse, shouting in Russian, and broke into a gallop. Though I was far from being a skilled rider, I dared not hesitate, for I could not leave Trotsky alone. So I whipped up my own horse and galloped off behind him, somehow staying in the saddle, my gun tossing against my side. The reason I was not killed is doubtless that I had a good, safe mount. After a while, Trotsky and I found ourselves on the road from Mexico to Taxco, where we continued at a full gallop until we reached the town. Trotsky rarely did anything as unexpected as this.

All Souls' Day is a popular holiday in Mexico, and during the thirties it was celebrated even more colorfully than today. On that day, festive crowds took to the streets, with firecrackers and articulated cardboard skeletons. Children nibbled ghoulish sweets — skulls of pink sugar, tibias of marshmallow. On the holiday afternoon of November 2, 1938, Diego Rivera arrived for a visit at the house in Coyoacán. Looking as mischievous as an art student who has played some prank, he brought Trotsky a big skull made of purple sugar, on whose forehead was written in white sugar, "Stalin." Trotsky said nothing, behaving as if the object were not there. As soon as Rivera had gone, he asked me to destroy it.

Diego Rivera had some great qualities. His vivid imagination allowed him to make penetrating remarks about people. But it was precisely in his attitude toward people that the erratic side of his character manifested itself most clearly. In judging a person he would fix on either one or another of several aspects and thus come, in the course of a few days, to opposite conclusions about that person. There was thus considerable fickleness in his personal relations. One morning, as I was having breakfast with Rivera and Frida at their house in San Angel, the mail arrived with a letter from an American writer. Rivera only looked at the name of the sender, crumpled the letter without opening it, and threw it across the room, shouting, "Ah, the swine, he has not dared to take a frank position on the trials!" A few days later, upon arriving at Rivera's house, I found him in the midst of a friendly conversation with the sender of the letter, who had written specifically to give notice of his coming. Such sudden turns in personal relations occurred constantly with Rivera.

The Mexican Trotskyite group numbered perhaps twenty to thirty active members. In spite of their small number, they were divided into factions, one of which centered upon Octavio Fernández, the other on

Galicia. Rivera kept by himself most of the time. He was also a rather special member of the organization, for the other members were young teachers or workers on extremely reduced financial means, whereas Rivera was a national legend, the sale of whose paintings earned him large sums of money. He generally provided for the financial needs of the group. When any step was being considered, such as printing a poster or holding a meeting, he could impose his will on the others, either by contributing immediately and generously if he was in agreement or by holding back if he did not like the project. Such a situation inevitably led to tensions inside the group. It would have been much better if Rivera had kept himself out of the daily activities of the group and had confined himself to being a generous sympathizer. But, no, he was keen on taking part in the inner life of the organization.

Trotsky's presence in Mexico did not make matters simpler. All of the active members of the group, whatever their faction might be, would take turns helping us to stand guard during the night. Every evening, two or three came to the house, and in the morning they left. Trotsky talked with them when they arrived, giving advice on the factional fights. The members of the group constantly felt the pressure of Trotsky's intervention in these matters. Because the situation within the organization was so chaotic, the International Secretariat and then the founding conference of the Fourth International had had to make decisions about the internal affairs of the Mexican section. At the founding conference, a resolution had been passed directing that the Mexican section be reorganized. The resolution stated: "As for Comrade Diego Rivera, the Conference also declares that, in view of the difficulties that have arisen in the past concerning this comrade in the internal relations of the Mexican section, he will not be a member of the reconstituted organization; but his work and his activity for the Fourth International will remain under the direct control of the International Secretariat." Rivera was not a man to accept with good grace decisions made from afar and without his direct participation. Such episodes created an atmosphere in which clashes were inevitable and frequent.

Trotsky often had conversations with Rivera about the activities of the Mexican group. The advice that Trotsky gave him varied over time. By the fall of 1938 Trotsky had probably come to the conclusion that Rivera should keep himself at a distance from the day-to-day activities of the group. But I do not know exactly what Trotsky told him, for I deliberately kept out of all their conversations on the subject. Anyway, such advice could only have provoked irritation in Rivera, whose ambition was to be a political militant himself.

Rivera's Trotskyism was also somewhat relative. Throughout my relations with him, he would often say, "You know, I am a bit of an anarchist." He would tell stories, which he had learned in Russia, about what had gone on behind the scenes in the early years of the Communist International, and the general import of these stories was that, even under Lenin, rather nasty things were happening. He would say nothing of this, however, to Trotsky, to whom he showed another face. In 1938 he wrote some articles about the countries of Latin America, in which he analyzed their situation and the role of the "sub-bourgeoisie," as he called them, with great penetration and brilliance.

What exactly were Trotsky's feelings toward Rivera? I can only give a partial answer to this question. After the infamies committed by the Norwegian government, Trotsky was grateful to Rivera for the efforts he had made in securing a Mexican visa. Rivera, although sick, had undertaken a long trip across Mexico to speak directly to Cárdenas, who was then on a tour. Trotsky was also grateful to him for the hospitality that Rivera had shown him in the blue house at Coyoacán. But there was more. Of all the persons whom I knew around Trotsky from 1932 to 1939, Rivera was the one with whom Trotsky conversed with most warmth and unconstraint. There were indeed limits that could never be crossed in conversation with Trotsky; but his meetings with Rivera had an air of confidence, a naturalness, an ease, that I never saw with anybody else. Trotsky was also happy that a world-famous artist had joined the Fourth International. One day, when my remarks had perhaps revealed a trace of skepticism about Rivera's political stability, Trotsky told me, not without a tone of reproach, "Diego, you know, is a revolutionary!" But at that time Trotsky may already have been trying to dispel some of his own misgivings.

The uneasiness between Trotsky and Rivera, with its crosscurrents of political and personal factors, began to take shape in October 1938, some time after Breton had returned to France. In addition to all the other reasons for disagreement, one of the underlying causes may have been the fact that Rivera's signature had been put by others, but with

Trotsky and Diego Rivera in conversation
at the house on Avenida Londres, Coyoacán.

his warm consent, to a document, the "Breton-Rivera" manifesto, of which he had not written a single line. But then we do not always know what is happening in the hearts of men. A further reason for malaise was Frida's departure for France at the invitation of Breton and Jacqueline, to spend a few months there. Rivera could not fail to feel a resulting imbalance in his life.

During the following weeks Rivera vacillated between two opposite attitudes. One day, he wanted to become the secretary of the Mexican Trotskyite group, though he was the least gifted person in the world to serve as secretary of anything whatsoever. The next day, he would speak of resigning from the group and even from the Fourth International in order to devote himself solely to painting. In mid-December Trotsky went to see him in San Angel. At the end of the meeting, Rivera agreed to speak no more of resignation, and the two interlocutors parted, apparently on good terms.

The incident that caused the explosion was a letter from Rivera to Breton at the end of December. When he had to write a letter in French, Rivera would ask me to help him. He would dictate the letter to me, and I would type it. On this occasion, he called me up and asked me to come to his house in San Angel so that he could write a letter to Breton. Soon after beginning to dictate, he phrased a sentence expressing criticism for Trotsky's "methods." I stopped writing. "Write! Write! I myself will show the letter to L.D.," Rivera urged. I had to make a decision. With any other person, I would have left. But the relations between Trotsky and Rivera were exceptional. Rivera was the only person who could come to the house at any time without previous arrangement, and Trotsky always received him warmly. With other visitors, there was always a third person present, most often me. But with Rivera, there was the possibility of loosening the close bond between Trotsky and me, against which he sometimes chafed, so I made a deliberate effort to keep out of their conversations. As I noted earlier, Trotsky once complained to me, "You treat me like an object." The relation between Rivera and Trotsky formed a sort of privileged sanctuary that escaped the system. I therefore accepted Rivera's declaration in good faith, preferring that he explain himself directly to Trotsky without my intervention.

After Rivera had finished dictating and before I left, he again told me that he would himself show the letter to Trotsky. "We will have it out," he said. I went back to Coyoacán and typed the letter, leaving a copy on the corner of my desk. Natalia would often come to my room, usually when Trotsky was having his nap, to read the letters and documents that Trotsky had dictated to me and which I had typed. She would do so whether I was in my room or not. On this day she happened to come in and find the copy of Rivera's letter to Breton, which she read. She then took it to Trotsky, and thus occurred the explosion.

Rivera's grievances against Trotsky's "methods," as explained in the letter, centered upon two slight occurrences of recent date. After publication of the manifesto signed by Breton and Rivera, a small group of the I.F.I.R.A. had been formed in Mexico, which had started to publish a magazine, *Clave*. At one of the meetings of the editorial board of the magazine, a young Mexican, José Ferrell, had been appointed secretary. Rivera, who was present at the meeting, had offered no objection. But in his letter to Breton he called this appointment a "friendly and tender" coup d'état carried out by Trotsky. The second episode was a last-minute decision at the printer's, without Trotsky's knowledge, to print an article by Rivera as a letter to the editor. Rivera imputed responsibility for this act to Trotsky.

Trotsky's reaction to Rivera's letter was to ask him, through me, to write a new letter to Breton, which would rectify the two misstatements. Rivera professed his agreement and made an appointment with me to dictate the letter. At the last moment, however, he canceled the appointment. He arranged for a new appointment and canceled that one also. He was obviously going through an emotional crisis. The words "friendly and tender" in his letter to Breton show that he was still attached to Trotsky.

With Rivera's refusal to write a new letter to Breton, the tone of disagreement sharpened. Trotsky and Rivera passed rapidly through the successive stages that, in a break, lead from friendliness to hostility. No further meetings took place between them. Charles Curtiss, who was the representative in Mexico of the Pan-American Bureau of the Fourth International, and I served as intermediaries. On January 12 Trotsky wrote a letter to Frida in Paris, in which he explained his version of the break. Frida, of course, stayed in Rivera's camp.

Feeling that he no longer was politically accountable to Trotsky, Rivera launched into a series of schemes with various small working-class groups, political and trade-unionist, that were more or less hostile to Trotskyism. Trotsky reacted violently. All bridges had been burned.

At that time the presidential electoral campaign was just beginning. According to the Mexican constitution, Cárdenas could not be a candidate again, and he failed even to get his party to accept a candidate of his choice. Rather, the army and business interests forced upon him the candidacy of Avila Camacho, who was subsequently elected. Múgica, the friend and closest collaborator of Cárdenas, decided to announce his own candidacy. He became, in relation to Camacho, the opposition candidate on the left. A third candidate, General Almazán, who was outside the government party, appeared as the opposition candidate on the right. The situation was so confused, by virtue of the fact that Camacho had been forced upon Cárdenas, that many *cárdenistas* voted for Almazán. In February, Rivera took an active part in Múgica's electoral campaign. Trotsky called that step a political betrayal. When Múgica later withdrew his candidacy, Rivera, according to some reports, supported Almazán. But by that time we no longer had any relations with Rivera at all.

After the break with Rivera, Trotsky could not remain in the blue house at Coyoacán. But it was not easy to find a new house right away, at a moderate rent and satisfying a number of specific conditions. As early as the end of January, Trotsky proposed to Rivera, through me, that he would pay him rent while I looked for a new place. Rivera refused, then accepted, then refused again. All this added more acrimony to the final phase of the break. Around March, I found a new house. It was in Coyoacán, and the rent was low, but the premises were in poor condition. In fact, the house, which was located on Avenida Viena, quite near the one that we were about to leave, was not currently occupied. It belonged to a family of storekeepers in Mexico City, the Turati, who had used it as a country retreat. The owners were happy to rent it, even to Trotsky. It had many positive features: enough rooms, a large garden, high walls, and surroundings that were easy to watch because the neighborhood was not yet built up. But repairs were necessary, some floors even having caved in. It also had to be furnished. A young Mexican Trotskyite, Melquiades, took charge of the work with the help of a few others. Not until the first day of May were we able to make the move from Avenida Londres to Avenida Viena. Trotsky transferred from one

*The house on Avenida Viena, Coyoacán, where Trotsky lived
from May 1939 until his death; in the foreground a brick guardhouse
is under construction for the Mexican police.*

house to the other on May 5. At the moment of leaving the blue house,
he placed on his now-empty desk two or three small objects that had
been presents from Rivera and Frida in better days; in particular, he
left a pen that Frida had given him, which he had used for a long time.

Trotsky felt at ease in his new abode. Once repaired, the house was
attractive, and it had a lot of space. The arrangement of rooms was such
that the part of the house in which he and Natalia lived was set well
apart, and they had privacy. Trotsky undertook to plant cactus. There
were even rabbit huts, and Trotsky took to feeding the animals in the
afternoon.

I have often been asked what role the 1937 affair between Trotsky
and Frida played in the break. Many questioners, with a knowing look,
led me to understand their opinion that this was the true reason for the
break. I must say that, on the surface, the role was nil. For one reason, I
was told by Frida that Rivera knew nothing of what had happened between Trotsky and her. An indirect argument is that, if the former
amorous relations between Trotsky and Frida had played a part in the
break, the rupture would have taken a very different form, since Rivera
was morbidly jealous. From everything I know, it appears that Rivera
had no particular suspicion. Of course, he may well have been caused

Trotsky and Natalia in the courtyard of the house on Avenida Viena, 1939.

Trotsky tending his rabbits, fall 1939.

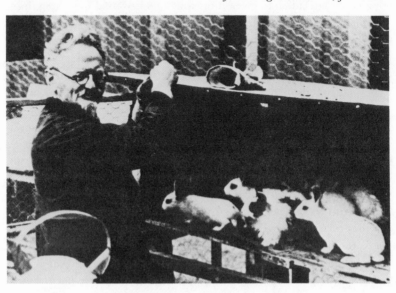

discomfort by Trotsky's intellectual superiority, but such whiffs of rivalry did not emanate from precise knowledge about what had happened between Trotsky and Frida, or even from faint suspicions about the matter.

A few years after the break between Trotsky and Rivera, and long after Trotsky's death, Rivera and Frida got divorced, then after a few months got married again. This conjugal crisis may have been provoked by what Rivera had learned, one way or another, about the past. His jealousy was extreme, despite the fact that he himself deceived Frida at every opportunity—or perhaps because of that fact. Such knowledge would also explain his bizarre political evolution. At the time of his break with Trotsky, Rivera's anti-Trotskyite tendencies took on anarchist and liberal hues in turn, but certainly never a Stalinist one. In fact, Rivera was the one who accused Trotsky of Stalinism. His going over to Stalinism, which occurred long after his break with Trotsky, may have been caused by an explosion of rage when he learned what had happened between Trotsky and Frida. Clearly, these thoughts are purely conjectural on my part, since I was then no longer in Mexico, but they are based on well-known facts which agree with my intimate knowledge of what happened earlier.

In June or July 1939, Trotsky asked me to do research in Mexico City's National Library and try to find some texts on the sixteenth century wars of religion and on the end of the Roman Empire. According to him, these two epochs of historical fracture were the ones to compare with ours. I can still see the scene in his study as he stood near me. I made some objections, mentioning the atrocities of the wars of religion, in which people were hurled down from towers onto the spears of soldiers waiting below. He gave me a look of rare sadness and said, "You shall see." We have seen.

During my work in the library, I found a quotation from Tacitus, who called Locusta, the poisoner hired by Nero, *regni instrumentum,* "the instrument of government." Trotsky used this quotation, concerning, I think, Yagoda. An echo of these preoccupations of Trotsky's are found in the last articles that he wrote, during the polemics of the American Trotskyite group, in which he touches the theme of socialism or barbarism. But I have the impression that his thoughts had advanced further than what he was then ready to put on paper.

*Trotsky with an American guard (Hank) during a picnic
in the country, 1939.*

One theme that often came up in the conversations, or even in the writings, of Trotsky was the charge that "old" people should not be trusted and that one should bank on youth. In his second article on Rakovsky's capitulation, written on March 27, 1934, he stated, "Let the sixty-year old fighter be replaced by three twenty-year old ones!" At lunch one day, probably in June 1939, he invented a kind of game, which consisted of identifying all the "old ones" who had left us. Trotsky counted them on his fingers. With each new name, he thrust out his forearm and pointed one more finger. Thus we dropped several names, one by one: Treint, Rakovsky, Van Overstraeten. Then I suggested rather shyly, for I did not know how he would take the name, "Rosmer?" He exclaimed in a strong voice, while thrusting out one finger more, "Rosmer!"

Alfred and Marguerite Rosmer arrived from France on August 8, 1939, bringing Sieva with them. It was the first meeting since 1929 in Prinkipo. A political break between Trotsky and Rosmer had occurred in 1930, when the former decided to back Raymond Molinier. During Trotsky and Natalia's whole stay in France, from 1933 to 1935, there had been no contact of any kind between them and the Rosmers. Yet now the Rosmers were warmly received. They settled down in the house in Coyoacán and took their meals with us. In conversation, Trotsky and Rosmer would discuss politics, but in a general manner. There was quite a precise line that they never crossed. The past was not mentioned, and the affairs of the French Trotskyite group were not discussed.

I remember one incident that took place at the end of August. Trotsky had conceived the idea of forming a special committee of the Fourth International, which would be honorary in character and would consist of well-known persons, even if those persons were on the periphery of the official Trotskyite groups. Trotsky mentioned Ch'en Tu-hsiu as a possible member of this committee. He was a well-known Chinese Communist, who had become a Trotskyite but had remained fairly aloof from the factional struggles that divided the various Chinese Trotskyite groups. Trotsky's project remained vague, and I am not sure that there are written traces of it. One afternoon, after Trotsky had called me into his study to tell me of his plan for the committee, he added, "Couldn't you ask Rosmer if he would like to be a member of the committee?" I

*Sieva, Marguerite Rosmer, Natalia, Alfred Rosmer,
and Trotsky in Taxco, August 1939.*

was surprised at the question, which was in fact extraordinary. Trotsky and Rosmer saw each other several times a day, so there was no need for a third person. They were also of the same generation and shared a common past that went far back, whereas I was of another generation. Moreover, Rosmer could not fail to realize that the question, coming from me, was asked at Trotsky's request, and Trotsky must have been aware that Rosmer would realize this. Ultimately, I spoke to Rosmer about the plan for the committee, and he agreed to be a member, though without displaying any particular enthusiasm. The entire project came to naught.

In September 1939 came the declaration of war. With Trotsky, I heard, on a short-wave receiver, news of the first torpedoing of a British ship by a German submarine. There was an air of *déjà vu*. Then began the "phony war." I sensed in Trotsky a weariness at witnessing the repetition of a catastrophe he had seen in 1914, but also a faith that in a few years the war would lead to the socialist revolution.

In October, Albert Einstein's name came up in a conversation between Trotsky and myself, in which Trotsky remarked, "He is essentially a mathematician." This, of course, was not correct, for Einstein's cast of mind was entirely that of a physicist. Whatever mathematical tools he needed, he took, already elaborated, from the works of mathematicians. Trotsky's remark was an echo of the discussions that had taken place in Russia around 1922, when an attempt had been made to show that Einstein's theories were in no way a threat to Marxist materialism, because they were somehow only mathematical fictions.

In October, my departure for the United States was decided upon. I had lived so many years in the shadow of Trotsky that I needed to be by myself for a while. I was supposed to spend a few months in the United States. After that, we would see.

I left the house in Coyoacán early in the morning of November 5. On the evening before, I had had my last conversation with Trotsky. We spoke about the situation in the American Trotskyite group, which was undergoing a serious crisis. The group was divided between a majority, centered around Cannon, and a minority, led by Shachtman and Burnham. Trotsky feared that Cannon, with whom he was politically allied, would tend to replace the discussion of political differences with organisational measures, thereby precipitating the expulsion of the minority.

"Cannon has to be held back on the organizational plane and pushed forward on the ideological plane," he told me. This was a little like the advice that he had asked me to give to Raymond Molinier in August 1933. In this last conversation, Trotsky gave me no actual "instructions" for New York, which my status as a newcomer would not have allowed me to apply. He simply explained how he saw the situation and in which direction I should move, according to my abilities. But by then, events had already run far ahead of us, and when I arrived in New York, the split was an accomplished fact.

About the months that passed between my departure from Coyoacán and Trotsky's assassination, I have little to add to what has already been published and is well known. I corresponded regularly with Trotsky, giving him information about what I had found in the American Trotskyite group after the split. The future murderer, Ramón Mercader, under instructions from the G.P.U., wooed a young American Trotskyite, Sylvia Ageloff, in Paris and became her lover. She was a good choice on the part of the G.P.U., for she had a sister, Ruth Ageloff, for whom Trotsky had considerable affection. Ruth, who had been in Mexico at the time of the hearings of the Dewey Commission, had helped us a great deal, translating, typing, and searching for documents. She had not lived in the house, but for a few weeks she had visited almost daily, to share our life and work. Trotsky had a very favorable recollection of her, so that a sister of hers could only be well received by him and Natalia.

A second link in the chain of circumstances that brought the murderer into Trotsky's study was the role of the Rosmers. Adolfo Zamora, who in 1940 had been a frequent visitor in the house at Coyoacán, told me in 1972 that the Rosmers, especially Marguerite, had been infatuated with Ramón Mercader. They constantly asked him for small services, which he was always ready to supply. In Mexico City and its suburbs, where transportation is difficult, Mercader made himself available at any time with his car to take the Rosmers one place or another. They also made excursions with him, such as picnics in the countryside, to which Sieva was often invited. Since Marguerite was very close to Natalia, this familiarity of Mercader with the Rosmers could not fail to give him some credit with Natalia and, therefore, with Trotsky.

There is one point that still puzzles me: why Mercader's way of speaking did not awaken suspicion in Alfred Rosmer's mind. Mercader claimed to be a Belgian. But as is shown by documents preserved in the Mexican courts, his French was sprinkled with Hispanicisms. A Belgian's French differs from that of a Spaniard. Rosmer, being French, knew the language thoroughly; he even wielded the pen rather well. So how is it that he did not sense something wrong in Mercader's speech?

In August 1940, I was in Baltimore, where I was teaching French. On the morning of the 21st as I was taking a walk, I passed a pile of *New York Times* newspapers stacked on the sidewalk and happened to glance down at the headlines. There it was, in the middle of the front page: "TROTSKY, WOUNDED BY 'FRIEND' IN HOME, IS BELIEVED DYING." I wandered the streets for a while, then waited for news on the radio. A voice announced: "Leon Trotsky died today in Mexico City." Darkness set in.

AFTERWORD

For seven years following Trotsky's death I remained active in the Trotskyite movement. By 1948 the Marxist-Leninist ideas about the role of the proletariat and its political capacity seemed more and more to me to disagree with reality. This was also the time when the full extent of Stalin's universe of concentration camps became known, at least to those who did not wish to close their eyes or stop their ears. Under the impact of this revelation, I began to reexamine the past, and I came to ask myself whether the Bolsheviks, by establishing an irreversible police rule and obliterating all public opinion, had not prepared the soil on which the huge and poisonous mushroom of Stalinism had grown. I pondered my doubts, and for several years the study of mathematics was all that allowed me to preserve my inner equilibrium. Bolshevik ideology was, for me, in ruins. I had to build another life.

APPENDIX

Correction of Errors
in Writings about Trotsky

These remarks are intended to correct errors in some writings that concern Leon Trotsky. They deal only with facts, not at all with opinions or ideas. Moreover, they do not pretend to be complete. New writings come out all the time, bringing their share of new errors or repeating old ones. My remarks are meant simply to warn the serious reader that great caution must be exerted in this field. The texts covering the entire exile come first, followed in chronological order by those dealing with a specific period.

Victor Serge and Natalia Sedova Trotsky. *The Life and Death of Leon Trotsky.* New York, 1975.

Long passages printed between quotation marks were written or dictated by Natalia Sedova. They contain valuable information, but apparently when Natalia wrote them, she had at her disposal no other documents than the file of the *Bulletin of the Opposition* and a few books. She did not have the opportunity of using the archives in order to refresh her memory. Hence these texts contain inaccuracies, in particular glaring errors of chronology. Moreover, to my knowledge, Natalia did not intend to have them published in the form in which they then stood.

Page 164: Change "Hoertel" to "Donzel."

Page 165: "He also began a biography of Lenin." The context suggests that this happened in Prinkipo, which was not the case.

Page 188: "Leon Davidovich had been asked to read a paper to a learned society there [in Copenhagen]." In fact, Trotsky had been invited by a students' organization.

Page 189: "We travelled through France by car accompanied by some friends. The Italian government allowed us to board a ship at Genoa, but when we got there Mussolini's police were in such a hurry to get rid of us that they tried to make us travel on a cargo boat." Many inaccuracies appear in these few lines. Natalia confuses Genoa with Marseilles and lays on the Italian government the blame for the vexations caused

Trotsky by the French government. Moreover, Trotsky and Natalia did not cross France by car, but by rail. "We spent the last few months of 1932 in an uneasy atmosphere, within sight of the Bosphorus. An accidental fire had completely destroyed Leon Davidovich's library and the whole of our collection of photographs of the Revolution." The fire did not take place in 1932, but on March 1, 1931. As for the damage wrought by the fire, see my text. The expression "within sight of the Bosphorus" is incomprehensible, since the Bosphorus cannot be seen from Prinkipo; one would like to see the Russian text.

Page 190: "She [Zina] was incapable of adapting herself to life in the West, and the loss of her Soviet citizenship had proved the last straw." This does not agree with the account given by Jeanne Martin, who was very close to Zina in Berlin and reported that Zina "did not at all want to return to Russia, quite the contrary."

Page 191: Change "Hoertel" to "Donzel."

Page 192: "[In Barbizon, Trotsky] shaved off his thick, grey goatee, so as to look like a middle-class French intellectual." Actually, Trotsky shaved his goatee in Saint-Palais, on October 9, one hour before leaving for the Pyrenees. In Barbizon, he let it grow again. It was a means of disguise that he kept in reserve, calling it "the last resource." He shaved his goatee again on April 15, 1934, just before leaving Barbizon for Lagny. Klement's "bicycle" was in fact a light motorcycle, what would be called today a motorbike.

Page 193: "At the end of 1933, we went into hiding in Paris for a few days." In April 1934, Trotsky went from Barbizon to Lagny for a few days, then from there by car to Chamonix. "For a few days a family *pension* sheltered us under the attentive eye of a *Sûreté* official." Here the chronological order is inverted, for this stay in the guest house took place before the residence in Saint-Pierre-de-Chartreuse. "Our residence permits were running out." The residence permits had been canceled immediately after the Barbizon affair, hence long before the stay at the Beaus' house.

Page 194: "We left the Beaus to spend some time in the dilapidated little house Leon Sedov and his wife had rented near Paris." This "little house" was a suburban house in Lagny, where Trotsky and Natalia lived for only a few days in April 1934 before going to the Beau house; here again the chronology is inverted. The Lagny house had been rented by Liova long before the Barbizon affair. It was kept in reserve, in case of emergency, and nobody lived in it regularly. Jeanne would go there from time to time. The inside of the house may therefore have been dusty, but the house itself was in no way "dilapidated." Trotsky and Natalia left the Beau house to go to Norway, passing through Paris, where they stayed a few days in the apartment of Dr. Rosenthal, the father of Gérard Rosenthal. All this is narrated by Trotsky himself in his diary. "Vandervelde's Belgian Government refused to let us spend even a day looking at the city's museums." Natalia is here confusing what happened in June 1935 with what happened in December 1932 during the return from Copenhagen. In fact, in June 1935, we moved perfectly freely in Antwerp. Trotsky had conversations with Belgian Trotskyites and other persons.

Page 197: Natalia places Rakovsky's capitulation to Stalin in 1935. In fact, it took place in March 1934.

Page 201: "Leon Davidovich had just finished *The Revolution Betrayed;* spring brought fresh new leaves, flowers, streams and clear, warm mountain air." The book was finished on August 5, 1936.

Page 211: "I tried not to lose sight of the only face I knew—Frida Kahlo's." Max Shachtman was also there, and Natalia had known him for years, whereas she had just met Frida for the first time.

Page 222: "With the exception of Albert Goldman, the Commission was made up . . . " Goldman was not a member of the Dewey Commission. He was Trotsky's counsel.

Page 228: The account of Rivera's telling Trotsky about Liova's death is overdramatized.

Page 251: "The light came in through a balcony window to which Leon Davidovich turned his back while working." This mistake by Natalia is incomprehensible, because she was obviously familiar with the arrangement of the study. Perhaps the translation of her text is not correct. Trotsky in fact had his back to the wall, the light coming from his left side. This study in the house on Avenida Viena is still arranged as he left it.

Page 253: Natalia places the Cedillo affair after the move to Avenida Viena. In fact, the affair took place in June 1938, when we were still on Avenida Londres in Rivera's house.

Page 254: "Rivera eventually strayed into General Almazán's Mexican Party." Though perhaps not erroneous in itself, this phrase is misleading. It seems to imply that this development was the reason for the break between Trotsky and Rivera, which was not the case.

Isaac Deutscher. *The Prophet Outcast: Trotsky, 1929-1940,* vol. III. New York, 1963.

Deutscher's book contains many factual errors. There are certain episodes that he was in no position to know about, and nobody can blame him for that. But what is surprising is that, in his accounts of such episodes, his narration is both detailed and erroneous. Even in the parts of his book based on documents, errors abound. Dates are wrong, which lead to inconsistencies, later patched up at the price of further distortion. My impression is that Deutscher worked hurriedly in the archives, more like a reporter who grabs any information than a historian who sifts documents. Two dozen names of persons and places connected with Trotsky, which recur again and again in Deutscher's book, are constantly misspelled. No serious student should accept a date or piece of information in his narration without first verifying it independently. There are few pages that do not call for some comment. The following remarks are only a sampling.

Page 8: Deutscher gives the impression that Trotsky went from the Soviet consulate in Istanbul to a villa in Prinkipo, which was not the case. "Prinkipo Islands" is incorrect; only one island was called Prinkipo. The date "7 or 8 March" is wrong. Generally, Deutscher makes a muddle of the question of Trotsky's successive residences.

Page 24: "He would go out for long trips, accompanied by two Turkish fishermen who gradually became part of the household." This statement falls somewhere between truth and fiction. See my text for the morning fishing trips. An overnight trip was the rare exception. The fisherman attached to the house was Kharalambos. During the first year, his father also came along from time to time. Neither Kharalambos nor his father lived in the house. Though formally Turkish citizens, both were Greeks. "The police guards, placed at the gate of the villa, attached themselves so much to their ward that they also became part of the household, running errands, and helping in domestic chores." I saw no such thing when I was in Prinkipo. In fact, we were careful not to increase our contact with the Turkish policemen beyond the necessary minimum. As for Trotsky, he was never familiar with them.

Pages 26-27: Deutscher mistakenly accepts the thesis that the Sobolevicius brothers were not trained G.P.U. agents but political defectors. "Trotsky's financial circumstances during the Prinkipo period were much easier than he had expected." This was true at the beginning, but certainly not at the end of Trotsky's stay in Prinkipo.

Page 59: Deutscher refers to "the American Mill." Mill (Obin) was a Jew from the Ukraine; he never set foot on the American continent.

Page 60: Referring to the factional fights in France, Deutscher writes: "The personalities were, as a rule, of so little weight, the issues so slight, and the quarrels so tedious that even Trotsky's involvement does not give them enough significance to earn them a place in his biography." Strange that a biographer should refuse to deal with problems to which his subject was devoting the better part of his time and energy.

Page 96: Deutscher calls Jakob Frank a "Trotskyist economist," failing to mention that at the time he may well have been a G.P.U. agent.

Page 149: Deutscher states that, after the fire, Trotsky moved to another house "until the Büyük Ada house was habitable again." Trotsky never went back to the Izzet Pasha villa.

Page 263: "He stayed in Saint-Palais from 25 July to 1 October." Trotsky left Saint-Palais on October 9, in the late morning.

Page 264: Trotsky met Spaak and Ruth Fischer not in Saint-Palais but in Paris, when he was already living in Barbizon.

Page 269: "He often received Fischer at Barbizon." Trotsky met Ruth Fischer in Paris; she never came to Barbizon.

Page 273: "The local *procureur,* followed by a platoon of gendarmerie and by reporters from Paris, came to interrogate Trotsky." There were no journalists with the district attorney. Deutscher confused court reporters with newspaper reporters.

Page 274: "He went to Paris and stayed for a few days with his son in a poor student's garret." See my account. The whole page bristles with inaccuracies.

Page 325: "The Minister of Justice ordered the deportation of Jan Fraenkel." Incorrect. See my account. Also, "Fraenkel" should be "Frankel."

Page 384: For the relations between Trotsky and Frida Kahlo, see my text.

Page 398: For Diego Rivera's announcement to Trotsky of Liova's death, see my text. Trotsky never "exploded with anger, and showed the door to Rivera."

Page 404: "It was not until October 1939 that the Rosmers at last brought him to Coyoacán." The Rosmers arrived in Coyoacán with Sieva on August 8, 1937. Deutscher's error is repeated on page 449.

Page 431: "André Breton . . . arrived at Coyoacán in February 1938." Breton arrived in Mexico City in the last half of April. Putting his arrival in February, at the time of Liova's death, leads to inconsistencies in Deutscher's narrative of events.

Page 432: "Breton's visit coincided with Lyova's death and the Bukharin trial." All this is false.

Page 444: Deutscher's account of Trotsky's break with Diego Rivera is totally wrong. See my text.

Page 477: "On personal grounds he [Trotsky] felt much closer to Shachtman" than to Cannon. This statement is not justified.

Francis Wyndham and David King. *Trotsky: A Documentary.* New York, 1972.

Page 126: In the photograph at lower left, it is apparent from Trotsky's features that the picture was not taken in Turkey. In fact, it was taken in Mexico, at the beginning of 1940, during a fishing expedition off Veracruz.

Page 127: "The Villa at Büyük Ada, Trotsky's home from 1929-33." Trotsky lived in this house from mid-January 1932 to July 17, 1933. See my text for Trotsky's various residences in Turkey.

Page 129: In the photograph, next to Trotsky stands Henri Molinier, with a beret, and in the back stands Jan Frankel, with a hat. In the text, "Oscar Cohn" should read "Otto Schüssler."

Page 132: "Pierre Naville and Raymond Molinier, who headed rival Trotskyist groups in Paris." Naville and Molinier were at that time in the same organization and would remain so for some years to come. "No boat to Constantinople was due for nine days, and they hoped for a little longer time with their son; but the French government were so anxious to be rid of their unwelcome visitor that he was hurriedly put on the first train leaving the country, which happened to be going to Venice." Not quite the truth. See my text. In the caption for the picture on page 133, change "1933" to "August 1933."

Page 133: "In July, the small and isolated International Left Opposition transformed itself into the International Communist League (Bolshevik-Leninist) . . . [Trotsky's] supporters there had renewed the campaign to get him a residence permit . . . This was conditional on his remaining in the south, never visiting Paris at all, keeping strictly incognito and submitting to police surveillance . . . [Trotsky] was spending most of the time in bed." All wrong. See my text. In right column, change "1 October" to "9 October" (twice) and "a month later" to "on 1 November."

Page 134: The phrase "hidden in a small park" is misleading. It would be more exact to speak of a garden. Moreover, the house was not far from the road and was perfectly visible from it. The house was not "guarded by sentries," Trotsky's destination was not "Paris" but "Lagny," and he was not "accompanied by van Heijenoort and Molinier." My text tells the whole story.

Page 136: Change "Louis" to "Lanis." Trotsky did not travel "in complete isolation, without any entourage." See my text.

Page 138: "Molinier was a frequent visitor to Prinkipo, and some embarrassment may have been avoided by the departure of Lyova and Jeanne." Since at that time Raymond Molinier went more often to Berlin than to Prinkipo, the conjecture is dubious. "Lyova's place at Prinkipo was taken by Zina—who was unable to fill it." Liova's place was taken by Jan Frankel. Change "January 1933" to "December 1932." "A week after his arrival" is incorrect.

Page 139: In the photograph caption, change "at Barbizon in November 1933" to "in Saint-Palais in August 1933."

Page 140: Change "thirty" to "sixty."

Page 142: "The Minister of Justice, Trygve Lie, ordered the deportation of one of Trotsky's secretaries, Jan Fraenkel." Not so. See my text. Also, "Fraenkel" should be "Frankel."

Page 143: "Trotsky remembered his friend Diego Rivera." Incorrect. See my text.

Page 150: In the photograph caption, change "Reba Hansen" to "Pearl Kluger." "Reba Hansen's husband Joseph was one of Trotsky's secretaries in Mexico." Not so at the time the picture was taken.

Page 151: André Breton "came to stay at the Blue House in February 1938." First, Breton never stayed in the house in Coyoacán. Second, Breton arrived in Mexico in the last half of April 1938.

Page 152: "But the civilized pleasure taken by Trotsky in Breton's society was brutally shattered by news from Paris." Breton's stay in Mexico took place several months after Liova's death.

Page 153: Liova was "persuaded by Etienne." The story is more complex. See my text.

Page 154: In the photograph caption, change "26 October" to "7 November." In the top picture, the four central persons are Rae Spiegel, Antonio Hidalgo, Natalia, and Trotsky.

Page 156: Change "early in 1939" to "late in 1939." Also, "to come out in open support of a candidate for the extreme right wing" is erroneous. See my text.

Page 157: The whole story is distorted. See my text.

Throughout the text, the following names are consistently misspelled: Ageloff, Cárdenas, Coyoacán, Domène, Frankel, Hønefoss, Wexhall.

Sara Weber (Jacobs). "Recollections of Trotsky." *Modern Occasions,* Spring 1972, pp. 181-194.

Page 181: "He [Trotsky] is losing his Russian secretary." Maria Ilinishna had no intention of stopping work. See my text. "I arrived in Istanbul early in May." Mid-June is more correct.

Page 182: "A high fence, electrically wired, surrounded the house." We had, alas, nothing of the sort.

Page 183: "Even simple walks were out of the question." At the very time of Sara Weber's arrival, Trotsky, instead of going fishing, often took an afternoon walk in the less inhabited part of the island.

André Malraux. "Leon Trotsky." *The Modern Monthly* 9 (1935): 37-41.

Page 40: "He spoke of Lenin, about whose work he is now writing." First, the translation is faulty. It should read, "He spoke to me of his *Lenin,* on which he was about to work." Second, there is an anachronism here. At the time of Malraux's visit to Saint-Palais, Trotsky was not yet contemplating writing a book on Lenin. His plans were quite different. Malraux carries backward what he learned later about Trotsky's activity. When Malraux wrote this article, in the spring of 1934, Trotsky had actually started to write his book on Lenin.

Page 40: "He was sixty years old and gravely ill." At the time of Malraux's visit to Saint-Palais, Trotsky was not yet fifty-four. Though at that time he had troubles with his health, he was far from being "gravely ill."

Jean Vilar. "Un Entretien avec André Malraux. *Magazine littéraire,* July-August 1971.

Malraux repeats several times that he met Trotsky in 1934. The meeting took place at the beginning of August 1933. In order to justify some of his views, Malraux says, "In 1934, Trotsky was writing his *Lenin,* and he thought of nothing else." A glance at the list of Trotsky's writings for 1934 disproves this statement. Malraux ceases to be honest when he states (if his words are correctly reported) that Trotsky thought "Spain should not be defended."

Jean Lacouture. "Malraux et Trotski." *Le Nouvel Observateur* 7 (May 1973).

"July 26, 1933" is erroneously given as the date of Malraux's visit to Saint-Palais. The date of Naville's first trip to Prinkipo is not 1932 but 1929.

Fritz Sternberg. "Conversations with Trotsky." *Survey,* no. 47 (April 1963): 146-159.

Page 146: "I came to spend about a week with Trotsky in France in 1934." Sternberg arrived in Saint-Palais in the very last days of August 1933 and left on September 2 or 3. Several times in Sternberg's text, "1934" has to be replaced by "1933."

Page 158: "The house in which he [Trotsky] was living was not guarded by police, although threatening letters were always arriving from right-wing extremists of the Action française." These extremists did not know, any more than the general public, where Trotsky was then living, and mail was not directly delivered to the Saint-Palais house.

Jean-Jacques Marie. *Le Trotskysme.* Paris, 1977.

Page 71: "Trotsky . . . took part in Paris, on August 27 and 28, in a conference." Trotsky did not leave Saint-Palais between July 26 and October 9, 1933.

Page 73: My name is erroneously included among the founders of *La Vérité.* I joined the Ligue in 1932.

Simone Signoret. *La Nostalgie n'est plus ce qu'elle était.* Paris, 1976.

Page 73: Yves Allégret "had been one of these four or five young men who acted as secretaries to Trotsky, in Barbizon." Incorrect.

Pierre Broué. "L'Action clandestine de Trotsky en Dauphiné (1934-1935)." *Cahiers d'histoire* 13 (1968): 327-341.

This is a serious piece of research, which rectifies the frivolous and erroneous statements made by Isaac Deutscher on Trotsky's life in Domène. I have only two comments. First, the statement, on page 327n3, that between the political events of February 1934 and the Barbizon affair on April 14, 1934, Trotsky would go "almost daily" to Paris is not correct. It would be more accurate to speak of weekly trips. Since Broué reports that for these trips, "Trotsky had shaved himself," his remark seems to apply to the period during which Trotsky was in Lagny, after the Barbizon affair. Before leaving Barbizon on April 15, Trotsky shaved his goatee, and he stayed for a few days in Lagny before leaving for the Alps. From Lagny, he could easily go to Paris "almost daily." Second, during his stay in Domène, Trotsky was still closely following the work of the International Secretariat, taking part in its decisions, and generally conducting a wide international correspondence. Trips between Paris and Domène were frequent. Liova, Jeanne, Raymond Molinier, and I went back and forth, each time carrying the mail that had arrived in Paris. None of this side of Trotsky's activities shows up in Broué's article; but perhaps that was not his task.

Fred Zeller. "Un Portrait du 'Vieux.' " *Le monde,* weekly digest, April 10-16, 1969, p. 12.

"He had succeeded in escaping until then forty-one attempts organized by his most ferocious adversary." Not one less, not one more. Why this mythomania, when reality is already so dramatic?

————· *Trois points, c'est tout.* Paris, 1976.

Zeller's account of his visit to Trotsky in Norway contains many passages that are striking for their freshness, naturalness, and accuracy. But he pads his text, mixing his memories with things that he has read. One must have an ear attuned to Trotsky's conversation to sift out what is authentic.

Page 101: "When he [Trotsky] was expelled from France in 1934 by the Radical government, he entered Norway in great pomp, received by the Socialist government with a flourish of trumpets, red flags and an immense crowd to acclaim him." Our landing on the Oslo pier was simple and banal. See my account. Besides, Trotsky left France in 1935, not 1934, and a "Radical government" was not then in power. The Norwegian government "separated him from Natalia." The Norwegian government behaved shamefully toward Trotsky, but stopped short of such an ignominy.

Page 104: "His elder daughter, Zina, killed herself in Germany, and so did the younger one." Careless writing. Trotsky's younger daughter did not kill herself in Germany; she died of tuberculosis in Moscow.

Page 124: Pivert "visited me in Barbizon." Pivert was never in Barbizon. Trotsky's meeting with Pivert took place in Domène.

Edmond Taylor. "The Rise and Fall and Rise of Leon Trotsky." *Horizon* 13 (Spring 1971): 34-43.

The "unidentified follower" in the picture on p. 43 is Antonio Hidalgo. The picture was not taken "in 1940" but at the beginning of 1937.

André Breton. *Entretiens,* rev. and corr. Paris, 1969.

Page 187: "This house was flanked, on each side, at some sixty yards, by two guard stations, where there were permanently five or six armed men whose mission was to stop all cars in order to inspect them." There was, in fact, a single guard station, a kind of cabin located in front of the house gate, on the other side of the street. The policemen who were there would not stop all cars that passed. They watched only the cars that did stop and the persons who came near the house.

Page 188: Trotsky's "mental organization . . . allowed him, for instance, to dictate three texts at the same time." I do not know where Breton ever picked this up—certainly not from me. In fact, Trotsky, who did everything in a diligent and concentrated manner, was irritated when anyone tried to push him into a situation where he had to do more than one thing at a time.

Museo Frida Kahlo, Coyoacán.

The house in which Trotsky and Natalia lived on Avenida Londres in Coyoacán has been turned into a museum. At the cost of false inscriptions ("Frida y Diego vivieron en esta casa 1929-1954"), everything has been done to erase all traces of Trotsky's stay in the house. The sessions of the Dewey Commission took place there, but nothing reminds the visitor of it. In the room in which Trotsky and Natalia slept for more than two years, somebody has left, as a turd, a small bust of Stalin.

INDEX